"The Future of Real Esta
professionals and those i:

It examines the major technical and social trends that will radically change how real estate will be bought and sold in the future.

The book also provides recommendations on how brokers and agents can profit from these changes, increasing their income by leveraging digital technology.

~Jeff Mindham, Real Estate Startup Writer

"Having spent thirty years in commercial real estate driving all over town searching for properties and delivering documents, the digital age brought a sigh of relief. However, it has forever altered the role of the real estate broker/realtor. The Future of Real Estate teaches us how to better utilize the digital tools now available to remain relevant in a rapidly changing industry so as not to be left behind in the dustbin of real estate history."

~ Denise Cassino,
Vice President, Colorado Real Estate Group

"What an AMAZING must read.. "The Future of Real Estate". Anya does an exceptional job in summarizing what one needs to do to EXCEL in the Real Estate Market. At the end of the day, you must "REINVENT OR DIE". This process of reinventing is always an ongoing process. Thanks for sharing your wisdom to enable others to grow exponentially."

~ Tony Berenyi,
PE, Founder of Berenyi Incorporated

"Anya's book opened an opportunity for my business growth that I previously overlooked. It increase my leads conversion by 8.5% per month."

~ Maria Serbina, MBA, Utah

"Long long time ago dinosaurs roamed the earth. A comet hit and the dinosaurs were gone. We have a new comet approaching the Real Estate industry. This comet is technology and if you believe that it will miss you, as the dinosaur, your business will perish. If you want to survive over the next decade, stay ahead of technology and your competition than THIS IS A MUST READ!"

~ Rafal Dyrda, The board of Directors Member at the Canadian Condominium Institute, Canada

THE
FUTURE
OF REAL ESTATE

EARLY WARNING REALTORS!

3 FUTURE TRENDS
That Every Realtor MUST Know to Compete with
ZILLOW, Convert More Leads and Double the Income

ANYA BARTHOLOMEW, MBA
FutureOfRealEstate.co

ISBN-13: 978-1975711146
ISBN-10: 1975711149

Edited by Jeff Mindham

Printed in the United States of America 1st printing – AUGUST, 2017

Anya Bartholomew, MBA

www.FutureOfRealEstate.co

Salt Lake City, Utah, USA

This book is dedicated to my mother

You believed and supported me
when I really needed you.
Your enthusiasm for learning and living fully
sparked my journey.

This book is also dedicated to my son Dima

You believed in my dreams.

ACKNOWLEDGEMENTS

To all clients and students

Thank you for sharing your stories, problems, experiences, feedback and suggestions.

It's my pleasure to get to know all of you over the phone, e-mail, Skype and chats.

Without of your guidance, my insights would have been short-sighted.

I am always happy to hear from you.

To my English Teacher

You invested your time into igniting my dreams.

Wherever you are, you gave me the wings to know everything is possible.

To my grandmother

You are my beacon of enduring and compassion

To my father

You gave me the gift of love and power

To my brother

You model compassion in the world around you.

Peter Diamandis

for curating exponential trends.

TABLE OF CONTENTS

INTRODUCTION **9**

SECTION ONE:
THE EXPONENTIAL TRENDS AND
THE FUTURE OF REAL ESTATE AGENTS . . . **13**

CHAPTER 1: THE FUTURE OF THE EXPONENTIAL REALTOR . . . 14

CHAPTER 2: THE EXPONENTIAL TRENDS 18

CHAPTER 3: 9 TRENDS THAT HAVE THE POWER TO DISRUPT. . 22

CHAPTER 4: THE SECOND DIGITAL REVOLUTION. 35

SECTION TWO:
AUTONOMOUS VEHICLES (AV) AND THE
FUTURE OF REAL ESTATE AGENTS. **43**

CHAPTER 5: THE DEATH OF CAR OWNERSHIP AND
THE FUTURE OF REAL ESTATE PRICES. 44

CHAPTER 6: ARE YOU A REAL ESTATE "UBER"
OR A REAL ESTATE "KODAK" 48

CHAPTER 7: FUTURISTIC CONSEQUENCES
OF AUTHONOMOUS VEHICLS (AV). 56

CHAPTER 8: REALTORS ALERT AND
AUTONOMOUS VECHICLES (AV) 61

CHAPTER 9: TIME FREEDOM, FUTURISTIC COMMUNICITES
AND REAL ESTATE. 65

SECTION THREE:
AUGMENTED REALITY (AR) AND
THE FUTURE OF REAL ESTATE AGENTS . . . **69**

CHAPTER 10: THE RISING TIDE OF AUGMENTED REALITY 70

CHAPTER 11: 100% DIGITIZATION OF REAL ESTATE 75

CHAPTER 12: "THE FUTURE OF THE REAL ESTATE" BUSINESS
MODEL 82

CHAPTER 13: 9 STEPS TO WINNING LEADS GENERATION. 85

SECTION FOUR:
ARTIFICIAL INTELLIGENCE (AI) & THE
FUTURE OF THE REAL ESTATE AGENTS . . . 91

CHAPTER 14: THE MIRACLE AND THE PROMISE
OF ARTIFICIAL INTELLIGENCE (AI) IN REAL ESTATE. 92

CHAPTER 15: ARTIFICIAL INTELLIGENCE (AI) FACT SHEETS . . . 98

CHAPTER 16: THE FUTURE WORLD OF ARTIFICIAL
INTELLIGENCE (AI) 102

CHAPTER 17: 9 STEPS TO GET STARTED WITH AI AND
DIGITIZE YOUR REAL ESTATE BUSINESS 107

CHAPTER 18: 9 WAYS ARTIFICIAL INTELLIGENCE (AI)
IS USED IN REAL ESTATE 111

SECTION FIVE:
THE FUTURE OF REAL ESTATE MARKETING. .115

CHAPTER 19: THE EXPONENTIAL REALTOR MINDSET 116

CHAPTER 20: WINNING THE GAME OF REAL ESTATE
MARKETING 123

CHAPTER 21: THE FUTURE OF MARKETING AND BRANDING . .127

BONUS: THE SECRET WEAPON OF LEADS CONVERSION 129

INTRODUCTION

Reinvent or DIE

"Our intuition about the future is linear. But the reality of information technology is exponential, and that makes a profound difference. If I take 30 steps linearly, I get to 30. If I take 30 steps exponentially, I get to a billion."

This quote is from Ray Kurzweil. His projections of future events are accurate ninety-four percent of the time.

Until December 2016, I knew nothing about the rising tide of technology because the signs of it had been blocked by my linear thinking, as I'm sure a few of you can relate.

When I stumbled upon this linear and exponential thinking quote by Ray Kurzweil, it evoked both urgency and presented two choices. The first was to continue doing what I have been doing, simply waiting for technology to disrupt my business. The second choice was to harness its momentum and potentiality to the fullest and double my income.

At the end of the day, the question always boils down to the ownership of personal power. Do we take control of technology and leverage its potential, or does technology control and overpower us?

This made me realize that exponential technology is bringing massive changes to real estate, and it's doing it very quickly. If I didn't deal with it now, it would be too late. As the noted motivational speaker Tony Robbins correctly said, "If we don't deal with those issues, they will deal with us."

I decided to be proactive, to take control, and to research how, exactly, technology is transforming the world's economy. And I moved quickly because these changes are coming fast. I didn't want to invest my time, energy, and money into shiny objects that would be obsolete in two years' time. I wanted to be ahead of the wave and leverage these changes and incorporate them into strategies for my business. I'm sure most of you can relate to that.

So, I put my MBA hat on and dove into what we called in business school a SWOT analysis, which stands for Strengths, Weaknesses, Opportunities, and Threats. After all, if this business assessment tool has worked for decades with other successful businesses, evaluating and then recommending industry best practices, it certainly seemed like a smart place to start.

My research and diagnostic analysis reinforced and validated my intuitive hunches. I remember being in the room with some of the world's most forward thinking entrepreneurs, watching, for example, the CEO of a large insurance industry company become totally unnerved. He had just determined that autonomous-driving vehicles would dramatically disrupt his business because they are so safe to drive. Soon, no one would need his insurance product. His business would become obsolete, like buggy whip makers in the age of autos.

As his emotional outburst unfolded before my eyes, shocking the audience of the world's best entrepreneurs, my mind raced; how might this impact the future of the real estate industry?

After leaving the event, I was viscerally, neurologically rewired. I now saw the future of the world very differently. Not only would the global economy be radically changed, but so too would the real estate industry. I also knew, in my gut, that just like the transportation industry was about to be disrupted by autonomously driven and electric cars, the real estate industry is next.

I couldn't explain this feeling, but my Clinical Hypnotherapy and Neurolinguistics Programming background told me to trust my intuitive business sense more than my logical, analytical mind. It was telling me "Now, the time to step up is now!" I simply knew the change was upon us and the magnitude of that change would be shocking.

Being a consultant who helps realtors and brokers maximize their production, I was profoundly affected by this revelation. For a month, I literally stopped every activity and dedicated all my time to doing deeper research and analysis to help me understand what was true and what was speculation.

The deeper I dove into researching technologies and their impact on virtually every sector of the economy, the more depressed I got. However, my eyes were becoming more open to things that I had previously blocked out of my consciousness or avoided altogether.

As I started noticing evidence everywhere of just how much technology was already disrupting virtually every business, industry, and even entire countries – the inevitability of rapid change was becoming more and more real to me. It also became apparent to me that society was not ready for these profound changes that were approaching it like a swirling tornado.

My primary concern was: how would people prepare themselves for this change that would result, for many, in the loss of their jobs? Would they see this change as good – probably not – and would they be prepared to help each other cope with this unsettling, rapidly approaching technical revolution?

For me, it became very clear: Reinvent or die.

SECTION ONE:
THE EXPONENTIAL TRENDS
AND THE FUTURE
OF REAL ESTATE AGENTS

CHAPTER 1:
THE FUTURE OF THE EXPONENTIAL REALTOR

By reading this book, you'll familiarize yourself with the major technological trends that, given their exponential nature, will be referred to as just that — exponential — throughout the remainder of this conversation. This will give you a bird's eye overview, the big picture in a comprehensive way, and it will alter your thinking. You will become less traditional and linear, and more innovative and exponential.

By the time you finish reading this book, you'll start thinking and acting exponentially, which will help you double your income.

Getting Ahead of the Game

As an exponential thinking Realtor, you will be able to see opportunities and threats that 99% of the traditional linear thinking Realtors will overlook. Because you understood how the exponential trends are reshaping every industry, every business as well as the national and global economy, you will understand, where others don't, that you must adapt to them because otherwise your income will be negatively affected.

Become an Authority, Celebrity & Expert

Exponential thinking will make you a bold real estate visionary, one who understands that by getting hands in the clay of exponential trends, you have the highest chance of not only surviving but also thriving and getting ahead. By keeping up with accelerating technological changes, you'll be outpacing your competitors and doubling your income.

This will happen because exponential thinking has the power to position and brand you as an Authority, Celebrity, and Expert in your local markets. This will put you on the map of the real estate industry in a big way.

Once harnessed, the rising tide of the exponential trends will raise your real estate boat so you can exploit lucrative opportunities and double your income. While your boat rises, most Realtor's will be sinking into the abyss of missed opportunities.

You will become a market leader

The issue of homebuyers who shop around for discounted commissions will be a thing of the past. Instead, these buyers will recognize the value-add you bring to the process – the true worth of the services you provide – no longer thinking about a lower commission, but instead they will become one of your brand advocates, raving to their friends and family about you.

And problems like chasing prospects who are looking for the cheapest realtor and trying to cut the commission will become history. Instead, you too could start charging for your services for what they are truly worth and working only with loyal fans.

If you are a broker, you could apply your new exponential thinking to address agent retention and recruiting challenges. This newly gained knowledge allows you to ride the wave of technology instead of being crushed by it. It will also let you more quickly and easily implement the right technology and to take control of your business and start working on your business, not in your business.

In other words, this new way of thinking will allow you to develop forward looking business strategies, not just small minded tactical adjustments.

Stop and think about. What is the average size of your commission? Imagine rebranding yourself as an Authority, Celebrity, and Expert in the digital real estate and generating just one more commission per month. And then doubling it again next month and so on. Pretty soon, those compounded commission increases will be sizable. How much more income would it be per year – a lot.

These annual compounded commission increases are EXACTLY the opportunity cost of rebranding yourself as an expert in digital real estate. New leveraging technology provides this "exponential doubling."

If you don't digitize your business, that annual doubled commission income is exactly what you will be leaving on the table. Harnessing the means of achieving "exponential doubling" requires that you immediately adopt a digitized real estate business model.

Those who understand this phenomenon tend to be like-minded and are attracted to each other like bees around a hive. The fact that they are clustered together fuels a collective momentum thus allowing everyone to achieve their highest goals and realize their dreams. I invite you to join the conversation in my Private Members-ONLY "Double Your Income for Realtors" Facebook Group.

Looking to the Future

When you start integrating and practicing exponential thinking, you'll find yourself making different decisions not just on a daily, monthly or even annual planning. You will be able to plan for the decade ahead. You can do this because, viscerally, you'll see the exponential (technological) trends before others do, and in a way that others don't.

And finally, you'll realize the danger of not arming yourself with exponential technology. When others Realtors do, they will fly past you.

Double Your Income

Everything you'll read in this book will do one of two things. Either it will inspire you to adopt new exponential thinking as a direct path to doubling your income, or it will make you remain a linear thinker, sleepwalking into the future, and suffering the consequences of that behavior.

And if I can awaken you to your true income potential, and help you double your income, then my intent will be fulfilled.

If any of this rings true, this book is for you, so keep reading.

CHAPTER 2:
THE EXPONENTIAL TRENDS

How to Stay Ahead

"The day before something is a breakthrough, it's a crazy idea."

— Burt Rutan, the man who designed and built SpaceShipOne.

How important is it to pay attention to these exponential trends? Nothing could be more important.

The real estate industry represents around 13% of the U.S. GDP. Understanding economic trends for a Realtor is critical; this is because they are an indicator of which way the nation's economy is moving, and that can impact your income. This fact particularly applies to entrepreneurs like us who have no job security. We are often at the mercy of economic trends.

If we invest time into understanding upcoming trends, we'll gain a long-term competitive advantage – a two-year head start — and we will know what others have yet to discover two years from now.

Armed with an understanding of trends, you'll have a much better chance of choosing the right technology for your real estate business. You'll get it right the first time and avoid the pitfalls of trial and error.

Recently, I had an opportunity to interview a successful real estate broker regarding the effect that trends had on his business growth and income. We were discussing the importance of trends first, strategy second and tactics third, when he confessed that two years ago, he looked into the international buyers' opportunities but failed to follow through.

Why? At that time, international buyers were only investing in commercial real estate. Overlooking the fact that commercial real estate is the trend that residential real estate follows resulted in a lost opportunity and therefore income.

If he had acted differently, our broker could have risen above his competitors, becoming an authority and gotten ahead, but he didn't.

If there is one critical lesson here, it will be the visceral understanding that trends have the power to position you as an Authority, putting you on the real estate map in a big way. Once captured, the rising tide of the trends could uplift your real estate boat towards lucrative hidden opportunities that can double your income. This is something that my research revealed to me that the majority of the Realtors fail to see because they are too busy working the today's deal.

Billionaire's Assessment Tool

Have you ever received the millionaire's advice that in order to become a millionaire, one must find the stream of money and get in the middle of it? If we follow that concept, we'll discover how the world's richest companies and investors are pouring billions of dollars into the 9 Trends.

How do they evaluate the most promising trends considering the fact that not all of them are created equal? Allow me to present the tool that has helped the wealthiest of investors double their billions many times over. It's short and sweet and it's about understanding the "investment cycle" of technology adoption and predicts when it's too early and when it's too late to invest.

Realtors often are attracted to trendy applications that are short lived. However, with this tool under your belt, your ability to discern between timely investments that will push you forward, and those that will lead you astray, will yield dividends for years to come.

If you're still not convinced, let me explain why you need to understand technology adoption cycles and add them to your exponential thinking realtor bag of tricks. It will make your decision making better, in terms of investing in technology. It will be more solid, clear, and you'll avoid the confusion of being bombarded with too much information and too many choices.

It will show you how much of a competitive advantage can you gain or lose by investing in specific tools, relative to other real estate agents and brokers.

The goal is to get in on the early adopters' opportunities that will allow you to double your income by catching up with the wave of innovation. This will truly put you ahead of the pack.

Phase 1: "Innovators": Representing 2.5% of the overall population. Innovators are eager to try new ideas and willing to take risks associated with new technology.

Phase 2: "Early Adopters": Representing 13.5% of the population. Early Adopters have the highest ability to act as opinion forms across all other adoption types.

Phase 3: "Early Majority": Accounting for 34% of consumers and an above average social class. The Early Majority adapts to new ideas before the average person.

Phase 4: "Late Majority": Also representing 34% of the population. The Late Majority approach new technology with doubt and skepticism, and in some cases, adoption is forced on them by network pressure.

Phase 5: "Laggards": These consumers are traditionalists accounting for 16% of the population. Their social class is the lowest of all groups, as is their financial power.

With that in mind, let's dive into the 9 trends.

CHAPTER 3:
9 TRENDS THAT HAVE
THE POWER TO DISRUPT

Exponential Trend #1
"Digitization: Connection and Communication"

✔ Rural internet services for 1.8 billion of new buyers and sellers of real estate.

✔ NEWEB Corp. plans 900 satellite internet systems, which represents 20% of 4,425 satellites needed for the entire world to go online.

✔ VIASAT plans the launch of a 3 "TERABIT" satellite capable of delivering 100 Mbps Internet to remote residential areas and gigabit speeds to commercial companies, aircraft & ships.

OPPORTUNITIES & THREATS: What are the overlooked opportunities and threats that will impact the buying and selling of real estate locally and globally?

How can you prepare today for 1.8 billion new buyers and sellers entering the global real estate market? Can Virtual Reality (VR), Augmented Reality (AR) and Artificial Intelligence (AI) help you connect with the global buyers anywhere on the planet? How could you become one of the few exponential thinking Realtors who are not only aware of this opportunity but also already leveraging emerging VR, AR, and AI technology trends? And how can you not only keep up with the game but also get ahead?

Exponential Trend #2
"Digitization: Autonomous Vehicles (AV)"

✔ Experts predict car ownership will be "DEAD" by 2025 because Autonomous Vehicle (AV) will cost less, be maintenance free, and eventually will become even more reliable, comfortable, and entertaining. Tesla announced their vehicles will be fully autonomous (self-driving) with 8 cameras, 12 ultrasonic sensors feeding deep learning computing platform in 2017.

✔ Hyperloop ONE OPENAIR test demo success; signs deal with Dubai Roads & Transit Authority to Cut Trip between Dubai & Abu Dhabi to 12 minutes. The "Hyperloop," a hypothetical high-speed transportation system that could shuttle people between Los Angeles and San Francisco in only 30 minutes. This speed is becoming a bit closer to reality.

✔ Self-Driving Trucks Deliver 50,000 Beers.

OPPORTUNITIES & THREATS: What are the overlooked opportunities and threats that will impact buying and selling real estate locally and globally within the AUTONOMOUS VEHICLES (AV) trend?

With the Hyperloop connecting Los Angeles and San Francisco, will it make Los Angeles real estate even more expensive, even higher than in San Francisco which is already the highest priced in the U.S.? Will the Millennial real estate buyer demand in Los Angeles drive San Francisco home prices even higher? As the new transportation continues to solve freeway traffic problems and Autonomous Vehicles (AV) make inner city communities cheaper and more enjoyable, how quickly will the 2nd Suburban Sprawl move away from the city center to the suburbs? And this is just the beginning because Texas just announced their intent to construct a Hyperloop too! What will happen to the transportation industry with car ownership predicted dead?

What will happen to the income and home buying habits of the estimated five million people head-of-household drivers and truckers? Will there be more foreclosures?

How can exponential thinking Realtors and brokers get in the middle of this emerging AV trend that offers unprecedented opportunities? It offers solutions to millions of potential sellers and buyer. And 99% of all Realtors and brokers are not even thinking about this.

Exponential Trend #3
"Digitization: Computation and Artificial Intelligence (AI)"

- ✔ AI predicts better than human: AI predicts real estate clients' preferences better than an experienced real estate broker.

- ✔ AI Beats Human Pilot in Air Combat: Air Force Colonel Gene Lee vs. "ALPHA" running on Raspberry Pi – $35. "Colonel Lee was not successful in winning against ALPHA. Not even once. Indeed, not even when the researchers deliberately handicapped ALPHA's aircraft, impeding it in terms of speed, turning, missile capability, and sensor use."

- ✔ AI predicts better than human: AI system beats 500-TO-1 ODDS, predicts the KENTUCKY DERBY TRIFECTA.

- ✔ AI predicts better than human: MogIA correctly predicted both Party Primaries and Trump's Presidential win in October. MogIA based its predictions on 20 million data points from Google, Twitter, Facebook, and YouTube.

- ✔ FUNNY: 19-YEAR-OLD CREATES AI THAT BEATS 160,000 PARKING TICKETS.

OPPORTUNITIES & THREATS: What are the overlooked opportunities and threats that will impact buying and selling real estate locally and globally within the trend of emerging artificial intelligence?

This is the primary trend that will affect real estate in a big way, and you can join the conversation in the chapter about Artificial Intelligence (AI) that is beginning to outperform humans in many areas, including real estate. What is the sweet spot of leveraging this trend to our competitive advantage? How do we deliver superior service and stand out in the competitive real estate world?

How can we get in the middle of this emerging trend that ninety-nine percent of all Realtors and brokers are not even thinking about?

Exponential Trend #4
"Digitization: Robotics and Workplace"

- ✔ 3D-PRINTED robotic hand mimics the human hand.

- ✔ FOXCONN replaces 60,000 employees in one factory with robots (110,000 out of 50,000).
- ✔ AMAZON GO STORE has no cashiers.

OPPORTUNITIES & THREATS: What are the overlooked opportunities and threats that will affect buying and selling real estate locally and globally within the trend of the robotic takeover of commerce?

How many factory workers, cashiers, and related fields will be replaced with robots and need help downsizing, selling their homes, and buying more affordable housing? Walmart employs 2.3 million associates around the world – 1.5 million in the U.S. alone and the majority of those jobs will be replaced by robotics.

A report conducted by PricewaterhouseCoopers LLP proves that retail powers the American economy. According to the study, retail is the largest private employer in the United States. Retail directly and indirectly supports 42 million jobs, provides $1.6 trillion in labor income and contributes $2.6 trillion annually to U.S. GDP.

According to fortune.com, job losses from robots could make universal income a reality. When robotics replace the majority of jobs in the retail sector, what will happen to the housing of those whose monthly income is disrupted? How will they pay their mortgages and rents? Which Realtors will they choose to work with? Probably the ones who have been preparing for this disruption and who are ready to help solve their urgent problems, relieve their pain, add massive value, while at the same time double their income.

How can an exponential thinking Realtor get in the middle of this emerging trend that 99% of Realtors and brokers are not even thinking about?

Exponential Trend #5
"Digitization: Materials, Manufacturing & 3D PRINTING"

- ✔ 3D-PRINTED houses in China, Russia, and the US are available in both low cost and high end.

- ✔ Combination 3D PRINTED material & living cells: Harvard scientists combine rat tissue with 3D printed gold to build 'living' biohybrid stingray.

- ✔ 3D bio-printed organs could be called the Holy Grail of additive manufacturing, and numerous research teams around the world are working hard to realize 3D printed implantable tissue – though virtually all experts believe it will take several years before patients will actually benefit from it.

- ✔ 3D-PRINTED sneakers by ADIDAS.

- ✔ 3D-PRINTED hair, brushes, and fur.

OPPORTUNITIES & THREATS: What are the overlooked opportunities and threats that will impact buying and selling real estate locally and globally within the trend of 3-D Printing?

Experts predict that we will start printing shoes and dresses by downloading designs from the Internet and printing them from home. What will happen to the manufacturing and the whole supply chain when producing apparel, storing and delivering products from the factory to the warehouse and to the retail store is no longer needed? What will happen to all those jobs, income, and mortgages along the entire supply chain in this industry? What if the Universal Income program that the leaders of all countries are discussing right now is not in place? According to motivational speaker Tony Robbins, if we as a society are not prepared to deal with those issues, they will deal with us. As Realtors and leaders in the community, we must take a bigger, bolder role in the transformation, preparing ourselves and those around us for the new world reality. What can we do today to make this transition into the technological renaissance of humanity a smooth, easy, and enjoyable ride for ourselves and others?

Exponential Trend #6
"Digitization: Diseases & Cancer"

- ✔ Artificial Intelligence (AI) saved human life: Watson looked at the patient's genetic information and compared it to 20 million clinical oncology studies determining that the patient had an exceedingly rare form of leukemia.

- ✔ Engineered T-Cell Therapy: Yielding "extraordinary" success on specific cancers: • 94% complete remission with acute lymphoblastic leukemia (ALL) • 80% of non-Hodgkin's Lymphoma • 50% of Lymphoma patients went into remission.

- ✔ CRISPR-Cas9 is a genome editing tool that is creating a buzz in the scientific world. It is faster, cheaper and more accurate than previous techniques of editing DNA and has a wide range of potential applications.

CRISPR used in humans: A research team at Sichuan University, China, used CRISPR to modify the immune cells of a patient suffering with an aggressive form of lung cancer and cured the patient.

OPPORTUNITIES & THREATS: What are the overlooked opportunities and threats that will impact buying and selling real estate locally and globally within this trend of accelerating breakthroughs in medicine?

According to Wikipedia, currently, 7.6 million people die from cancer worldwide every year, of which 4 million people die prematurely (aged 30 to 69 years). Each year there are approximately 4 million births in the U.S. and 2.4 million deaths. When this ratio of birth and death shifts, will the demand for houses shifts as well? Where in your area will the spike in housing demand drive up housing pricing? What are the suburban areas in your real estate market that are most likely to attract this demand? How can we get in the middle of this emerging death rate decline trend that ninety-four percent of all Realtors and brokers are not even thinking about, but fortunately this book is preparing you for?

Exponential Trend #7
"Stem Cells and Longevity"

✔ Young blood experiments and longevity. *Nature* reports, "In the heart, brain, muscles and almost every other tissue examined, the blood of young mice seems to bring new life to aging organs, making old mice stronger, smarter and healthier. It even makes their fur shinier."

✔ Aging is reversible in human cells and live mice. Researchers at the Salk Institute were able to turn adult cells back into embryonic-like ones, in both aging mice and in-vitro human cells, extending the life of a mouse. Human trials expected within ten years.

✔ Stem cells help stroke victim walk again, and allow paralyzed victim to use arms again.

OPPORTUNITIES & THREATS: What are the overlooked opportunities and threats that will affect buying and selling real estate locally and globally within this trend?

When a population lives significantly longer, and maybe, as some experts predict, as long as people want; how will it reshape demographics of buyers and sellers in your area? Will more kids live with their parents or will they move in with people who share their common values and interests? Will local communities start gravitating towards psychographics more than demographics, especially if we factor in Universal Qualifying Income? Will we see the rise of artistic, religious, and political communities spending more and more time together? Facebook and Google are already building mini-cities inside and around their facilities that provide in-house day care, gyms, healthcare and more. Will this become the new community building model? And if so, what can an exponential forward thinking Realtors and brokers do today to take advantage of the early adopters?

What are the overlooked hotspots of buying and selling within this trend of a population that will live longer and perhaps in the same house?

How will reversing of aging change our families and communities?

Where will the age-reversed population prefer to live?

How can we get in the middle of this emerging trend that ninety-four percent of all Realtors and brokers are not even thinking about?

Exponential Trend #8
"Digitization: Renewable Energy"

✔ Renewable energy is finally cheaper than coal. According to *World Economic Forum Reports*, "Solar and wind is now the same price or cheaper than new fossil fuel capacity in over 30 countries."

✔ Energy experts are likewise telling us that coal will not recover because renewables are cheaper than coal.

✔ Elon Musk announced that Tesla announced Solar Roof Tiles that look better, last longer, have better insulation and actually have an installed cost that is less than a normal roof plus the cost of electricity.

OPPORTUNITIES & THREATS: What are the overlooked opportunities and threats that will affect buying and selling real estate locally and globally within this trend?

Will houses without solar roofs be harder to sell? Will those with it be appraised higher, become more desirable and sell faster? Will the option to finance a solar roof into the mortgage attract on-the-fence buyers who are Green planet conscious?

How can you prepare today for the jobs in the coal industry that are being disrupted? Will the loss of income of the head of these households spike foreclosures in the coal dense states, cities, and neighborhoods? Will you be the only Realtor in the area who has been preparing those families for the transition into the Universal Qualifying Income (UBI)? Will you be the only real estate professional who has been developing and conveying unique marketing content that bonded them with you for life? They will refer their friends and family to work with only you.

How can we take full advantage of the opportunity to add value, relieve pain, and double your income? Ninety-four percent of all Realtors and brokers are not even thinking about this because they are too busy to evaluate ripe fruit opportunities that are available.

Exponential Trend #9
"SPACE & PHYSICS"

✔ Elon Musk, the founder, CEO, and CTO of SpaceX announces HUMAN TO MARS MISSION as soon as 2024.

✔ Breakthrough Starshot project by the famed cosmologist Stephen Hawking targets for humanity to reach the stars. Stephen Hawking, along with a group of scientists and billionaire investor Yuri Milner, unveiled an ambitious new $100 million project, which aims to build the prototype for a tiny, light-propelled robotic spacecraft that could visit the nearby star Alpha Centauri after a journey of just twenty years.

✔ EVIDENCE FOUND FOR PLANET NINE. Planet Nine is believed to be an ice world some ten to fifteen times the size of Earth.

✔ The universe determined to have 2 trillion galaxies, which is 20x the number previously believed.

4 Myths of a Linear Realtor

MYTH #1. If our cognitively biased mind is saying "this too shall pass" and we pay attention to it, then we have lost the VR and AR game in advance. Microsoft, Apple, Google, Amazon are investing billions of dollars in both AR and VR, and they are expecting exponential rewards. Why not follow the money flow?

MYTH #2. "It's too early." If you believe this to be true, go to Amazon and search for AR devices. You'll see for yourself how many products are already on the market at different price points and under different brand names. And the truth is... If your Sphere of Influence doesn't see you as the VR and AR expert, they are likely to transfer loyalty to the other Realtors who haven't missed this opportunity. Why wait?

If you are still reading, then you are likely open to VR and AR, but might still feel undecided. You are not alone. Six months ago, I didn't know VR and AR existed because I had been on a mission to unplug from negative news for twenty years.

However, once I realized how fundamentally VR and AR are going to change our lives, my survival instinct kicked in and I went into panic mode. Gradually, I reframed survival into freedom of choice and owned the power that this futuristic evolution affords.

MYTH #3. "My real estate business is different and technology-driven brokers don't understand the nature of real estate." "My business is different" has been a popular self-sabotage among entrepreneurs. Simply start with your diagnostic process and measure your objective against the best business practices in digital real estate.

MYTH #4. "I can't do anything about it anyway, why bother." If we don't believe we can do something about the reality around us, then we don't exercise our godlike powers. Instead, why not ask better questions. In how many ways can I reap the benefits of this once in a lifetime opportunity present for my business, my clients, and the world at large?

Why not adopt the "can-do-a-lot-about-it" attitude and stop feeding fear, which causes us to delay and postpone what is good for us? We are not tools in the garage, but rather we are humans with the right to do something about a lot of things (far more than we do right now), so why not give it a shot?

CHAPTER 4:
THE SECOND DIGITAL REVOLUTION

The way technology is about to change everything we consider normal is similar to the time when humanity went from a computer-less society to one where everybody has one. Today, most of us have either a desktop, a laptop, a tablet or a cell phone. The widespread use of computers has resulted in an avalanche of digital conversations between clients and Realtors. It is rapidly becoming the preferred means of communication, much more so than face-to-face interactions.

Millennials, for example, receive 80 messages per day on average, which is one every eight minutes, and they represent the future.

Today, we have 105% more cell phones in the U.S. than the actual population, which means there are 317,874,628 cell phones nationwide. In China, that number of cell phones over the population is 155%. And cell phone rate of ownership is not slowing down, but rather accelerating.

Every night, we go to bed and wake up with a few mobile computers by our bedside. We spend 1.8 hours per day on mobile screens and 55-minutes per day on Facebook. The average American under the age of 45 receive 85 text messages per day, and 95% read them in less than three minutes.

With the digital Internet and mobile computers, we have access to more knowledge than the President of the United States had twenty years ago. In a way, technology has already made us "super humans" and almost cyborgs, according to Elon Musk.

Can you even remember the time when we lived without computers? How many individuals in the early '90s thought the Internet was nice but had nothing to do with making money? Yet, in a time of the first Internet Revolution, there were exponential thinkers who did not succumb to complacency, reinvented themselves and their businesses, added value to millions of customers and, as a consequence, made billions of dollars in profits.

What stops us from reinventing ourselves and taking full advantage of the Second Internet Revolution that will be even bigger than the first?

As Jeff Bezos, CEO Amazon put it, "You have to be willing to be misunderstood, if you are going to innovate." He is today one of the wealthiest men on earth with a net worth estimated at $85.7 billion. Bill Gates follows close behind as does Mark Zuckerberg of Facebook.

Digitization and Dematerialization

We are rapidly digitizing and therefore dematerializing reality as we know it. The material objects of the old "reality" are disappearing, while digital objects are moving into our living spaces. With time, the digitized objects will become more real and what we see right now will become more digital, even though those two parallel universes once existed in two different dimensions.

We are beginning to experience digital objects spinning out of computers and into our "reality." We are beginning to experience people teleporting into different spaces through augmented reality. We're beginning to experience information in a very, very different way.

> "With the advent of sensors, with the advent of artificial intelligence and the advent of the computer, for the first time ever we are able to intercept these two universes and mix realities that try to define the intersection between the analog and the digital, between atoms and bits, between what is real and what is virtual by essentially merging the positives of both universes. The fact that it is immersive, the fact that it is connected in real time while maintaining the ability for us as humans to now have the super power to displace space and time."
>
> — Alex Kipman, Microsoft HoloLens co-inventor, who has his name on 150 patterns.

Demonetization is the byproduct of dematerialization and digitization and the movement towards the economy without money in the future. But to get to this future, businesses, industries, and economies, as well as individuals, must survive the unprecedented leap from material in a digital world.

Did you know that Finland launched a Universal Basic Income (UBI) experiment? Obviously, they are ahead of the game. Ty realized that the lost jobs from the 9 Trends would require a monetary cushion to avoid economic disaster among unemployed families who are not prepared for the transition.

After all, it's not easy to orient yourself to the new worldview where old economies and industries are disappearing, unless you are staying ahead of the game. Finland is proactively staying ahead and reinventing the economy and the very nature of money, and they are inviting others to do the same. Their UBI trial will give out $587/month, tax free, to 2,000 randomly selected Finns.

In the case of money, the proof is the rapid acceleration and adoption of bitcoin. What is a bitcoin? According to Google, it's a type of digital currency in which encryption techniques are used to regulate the generation of units of currency and verify the transfer of funds, operating independently of a central bank. Many banks and industries, including future thinking real estate brokerage, are adopting it today to prepare for the future.

Where do the jobs and industries disappear to? In the digital economy, digital computers, digital data, digital objects, digital relationships all exist, and much more. We already live in a more digital world than we realize.

Do we live inside the computer?

Have you ever watched the movie *THE MATRIX* and wondered why their fans were lining up the night before for the release of the next Matrix series? Have you ever watched *The Truman Show* and had a funny feeling that it might be you who is being watched or as if you are a show? Have you tried falling asleep, telling yourself that you are should wake up; however, when you wake up you're actually asleep?

If you haven't done all of that, you must have done some of it. The fact is that millions of people continue to watch *THE MATRIX* and ponder whether it's true? I recently posted the question on Facebook "Honestly, how many times you watched *THE MATRIX*?" The winner said they watched 251 times. The amount of engagement on this one post was over a 100.

If *THE MATRIX* is of interest to you, you are not alone. Recently Elon Musk was asked the question if he believes we might be living in a computer simulation.

His response was that he's thought about that a lot and endlessly discussed it with his brother. The thinking behind that was the progression from the first video game that initially had only a dot and a square, to the fully visceral 3D Virtual Reality games that are played by thousands of people simultaneously. That made Elon realize that in another 100 years, the scale of the video game might as well be the size of the EARTH.

Elon Musk also added that the chance that we are NOT inside the computer simulation is one in a billion.

If you go to YouTube and search "Elon Musk and simulation theory," you'll have fun. You'll also notice that it has over a million views.

Elon Musk is not alone in his realization of a simulation theory. Recently, I attended an event with Peter Diamandis, the co-founder of Singularity University. At the event, the audience asked him, "Elon said it's a simulation. Do you believe it's a simulation?" The response was, "Yes, I believe we live in a simulation, but it does not change anything." A great answer and a practical one, too.

Recently, I was watching people live when experiencing the VR walking the plank game. A tall, strong guy put on the VR glasses, started walking the plank and then... he started shaking and looking highly stressed. Then I watched the girl put the virtual reality goggles on, who also started walking the plank and then.... She started shaking, falling, and screaming.

I got curious and decided to see for myself how a pair of googles could cause an instant neurological stress. Then, the instructor put the goggles on me and said "Look up, " and I looked up, and there was the ceiling, and then I looked down and then there was the flooring. Then suddenly the ceiling became the blue sky and the flooring dropped away and became the abyss of the Grand Canyon, with a less than a foot plank for me to cross.

I was standing there for a few minutes with a visceral animal fear rising and tried to walk the plank but couldn't. At that moment, the whole simulation theory became real for me.

Consider this. What if the physiology of a body is actually a sophisticated VR google? Ray Kurzweil, when presenting to the attorneys in London about future trends, explained how it is now obvious to scientists that health and medicine "are" an information system; this makes even more sense.

Another fact that we are 3D PRINTING human organs, like livers and hearts, points in that same direction. And there are case studies where those organs are successfully adopted by the body.

Simulation or not, let's get back to playing this game full out. In order for us to do that, we must start by reinventing ourselves. Let's game.

What Can We Borrow From Elon Musk

Before we get into the rules of the game if reinventing real estate best business practices, let's start with reinventing ourselves by modeling Elon Musk.

Did you know why Elon Musk, CEO of Tesla left Stanford University after two days where he was a student pursuing his Ph.D. in Physics? According to Elon Musk, the Ph.D. could wait, but the opportunity cost of missing out on the Internet revolution was a once in a lifetime opportunity too good to miss.

The world famous futurist, inventor, and entrepreneur Elon Musk saw a vision of what's possible with the 1st Internet Revolution. With his brother Kimbal Musk and $28,000 of their father's money, Elon Musk started an internet technology company Zip2, which provided online city guide software for newspapers.

In February 1999, Compaq Computer offered $307 million to acquire Zip2. Elon and Kimbal Musk netted $22 million and $15 million, respectively.

Then Elon Musk repeated the process again and cashed out $180 million dollars from his second internet startup PayPal.

That led him to become the founder, CEO, and CTO of SpaceX; co-founder, CEO, and product architect of

Tesla Inc.; co-chairman of OpenAI; founder and CEO of Neuralink. He was previously co-founder and chairman of SolarCity.

As of May 2017, Elon Musk has an estimated net worth of $15.2 billion, making him the 80th-wealthiest person in the world. In December 2016, Musk was ranked 21st on *Forbes*' list of The World's Most Powerful People.

We all have an Elon Musk within. It may be on a different scale, but we all have the potential that hasn't been harnessed yet. How do we harness it to convert more leads into closed transactions that will double our income?

The answer to this question is even more urgent than we realized because we are on the tipping point of the 2nd Internet Revolution. And the opportunity cost of a lifetime is too illogical to miss. And that brings us to grasping the rules of the 2nd Internet Revolution game.

SECTION TWO:
AUTONOMOUS VEHICLES (AV)
AND THE FUTURE
OF REAL ESTATE AGENTS

CHAPTER 5:
THE DEATH OF CAR OWNERSHIP AND THE FUTURE OF REAL ESTATE PRICES

How to Spot a Billion Dollar Idea

We've just talked about the second internet revolution rushing into the real estate business, and now we can explore what specifically is poised to change faster than we can imagine—and how it will impact real estate in a way that we haven't realized. Are you ready for a conversation about Autonomous Vehicles (AV)? Buckle up.

The innovation-driven Uber business model is at the heart of Autonomous Vehicle (AV) Revolution with its million Uber rides per day worldwide domination. What is interesting about Uber is that it didn't start with a billion-dollar business, but rather with a billion-dollar idea. When in Paris, the owner of Uber was wishfully thinking of an app where users could push a button and a car would magically appear.

This simple Parisian daydream evolved into the multibillion-dollar ride company, timed perfectly to meet the market's demand for a convenient transportation service in a moment that marked the tipping point in demand for a prompt, reliable, and cheap car service that leveraged the frustrations toward the taxi industry.

Take Inventory

To create your own billion-dollar idea, consider asking yourself: *"What am I not seeing right now that could add value to millions?"* This inventory will help you anticipate the actions of your business and help you develop a robust strategy to guide you in the future.

Peaks and valleys are nearly instantaneous in a rapid-fire economy where companies, industries, and even countries are being re-evaluated from the perspective of *"who offers the highest value to the end consumer."* The industry term for this notion is "deceptive disruption," with the acceleration of exponential technologies driving changes in markets which are following the S-curve of doubling, often referred to as "Moore's Law."

A real estate leader utilizing new opportunities rides the wave of technology and harnesses its doubling curve, while those falling-behind brokers are still undecided. Waking up to the game of doubling tomorrow — might be too late.

You have to agree that the benefits of this seemingly insignificant Paris idea shouldn't be underestimated. Uber has now truly revolutionized not only transportation but multiple companies across several industries. It's quite a start for a bit of "wishful thinking." Inspiring to say the least!

Real estate is in the direct zone of fire

This chapter will explore opportunities and threats for those realtors and brokers who are sitting-on-the-fence and are still unsure where to start. We aim to offer you food for thought and some ideas on how to begin. This valuable section will help those already moving forward with a complementary perspective to spot overlooked opportunities because blind spots are our common enemy.

The book is written as a survival guide for the real estate agents of the future. The expectation is that the more you use this book—even a year after finishing it—the more you'll find useful predictions and assumptions for building a long-term real estate brand strategy: you'll align yourself on the ladder of success, leaning it against the longest-lasting and highest paying real estate wall of thriving success.

Focused Energy

Think back to your childhood and taking a magnifying glass outside on a sunny day. Do you recall using that magnifying glass to focus the energy of the sun onto a piece of paper? Amazingly, you could burn a hole in the paper using that tool. There's no effect on the paper without the magnifying glass. However, leveraging the right tool is critical to a task, and learning more about Autonomous Vehicles (AV) will help you focus your efforts to help you build a long-term brand strategy that will continue to double your income for years to come.

Leveraging your toolkit will help you consistently add to your brand's core strength and build even greater momentum. That's not baiting and switching from one shiny object to the next, but saving your time and foregoing unnecessary financial investments for greater efficiency and effectiveness for your business. All concepts in the AV chapter are principles rather than tactics, which build a solid foundation for the double growth in your real estate business.

So, if you are serious about becoming a "real estate Uber," consider building your future-proof brand's foundation by following their timing model. That model is based on "sooner rather than later." This is truly how Uber runs its business...just ask their drivers. They believe that the minute Uber comes up with a new idea, they instantly test and drive it into implementation.

Love and Fear

Experts believe that two primary forces drive human behavior: "love" and "fear." With that in mind, ask yourself:

- ✔ Is it possible that delaying your own million-dollar ideas is caused by fear?

- ✔ Is it fear that activates self-sabotage and leaves us spinning our wheels by engaging in strategies destined to fail?

How often do we actualize self-fulfilling prophecies rooted in fear?

Don't fall into that trap. Instead, start noticing fear, choose inner power, and act boldly now.

We can learn a great deal from Uber, primarily the principles and behaviors that will help us double our income. Those ideas will help navigate our business into smooth waters of the technological renaissance and away from disruption. Let's consider how we can become the force that facilitates the transition into the second internet revolution—not only for ourselves but for our neighborhoods and communities.

CHAPTER 6:
ARE YOU A REAL ESTATE "UBER" OR A REAL ESTATE "KODAK"

Did you know that Uber proved a billion dollar evaluation on the same day Kodak filed bankruptcy? And the main reason is Kodak's complacency and Uber's futuristic drive for innovation. To avoid becoming a real estate "Uber", why not consider 5 Lessons from Uber.

UBER LESSON #1.
Long-term strategic planning

Uber is aligning its annual tactics with long-term strategies and vision. Do you have a long-term strategy and vision with which you align your annual tactics?

Uber is heavily investing not only in an Autonomous Vehicles (AV) that have already started driving in San Francisco but also into a VTOL (Take-off and Landing) fleet with an aggressive deployment forecast. This decision is based on their research that lets them know how future cities will feel, look, and sound. Most importantly, they know how these future technologies will impact the redistribution of the real estate supply and demand in both large and small-scale cities.

"I would not want to be in the parking lot business," said Peter Diamandis, the world-renowned futurist who curates content for millionaires and billionaires.

Why would he say that?

Recently, a real estate investing firm was noted because of a brilliant, rock-solid tactical strategy. The firm had established offices in Tennessee and North Carolina, and was planning to open an office in Utah.

Why Utah?

Their agents couldn't cite the golden tagline from the national newspapers: "High-tech Mecca rising in Utah to rival Silicon Valley," but the thought leaders in this company were three steps ahead examining the next areas of growth in the industry.

The implications for real estate are brilliant, yet if you are not aligning your tactics with the trends, you are working harder, for longer hours, and getting leftover clients.

UBER LESSON #2:
How Can Uber Disrupt Our Plan?

It's shocking, but one of the questions Uber consistently asks themselves is, "How can we disrupt, dematerialize, demonetize, and democratize our business model?" Truly a billion-dollar question that could help any business owner uncover blind spots and identify overlooked threats to adjust its strategies before it's late. This is why Uber is deploying Autonomous Vehicles (AVs) to stay ahead of the curve, even though they are simultaneously disrupting the jobs of their own drivers. If they don't do it first, their competitors will, and Uber will go out of business.

Have you asked yourself this question: "How can I disrupt, dematerialize, demonetize, and democratize my business model?" It's how you will stay ahead of the game.

UBER LESSON #3:
What Makes Uber Future Proof?

One of the things that makes Uber a strong player in its industry is that it clearly outlines the company's mission and critical values. With these statements in hand, when a tough business decision arises, every person on the team will know exactly why the company made the decision it made. Think about how your team would react to a tough business decision or a bold change if you made it tomorrow. Are your brand's values and priorities clearly defined and communicated to everyone on your team?

This brings to mind the rocket launch metaphor: If the launch pad for your business rocket is wishy-washy and unstable, how far do you think your rocket will fly?

Interestingly, Uber fashioned the core values of its company culture to be rock solid and then communicated those beliefs to every employee. When a tough decision is made based on those values, the team is united and carries the Uber ship into waters where nobody has ever been before — effectively.

Think about what it would take for your business to do the same. Think of how much more effectively your team would operate as one unit in the rocky waters that make up the transition into abundance? What are you going to do about it today?

For Uber, when questioned about the moral obligation to the disrupted drivers who are replaced by the autonomous vehicles, they'll have a rock-solid map to navigate those stormy waters and the ability to breathe reassuring confidence. You can do the same for your team and for those around you, one person at a time.

UBER LESSON #4:
The End User Supremacy

Uber's business model is aligned with the main value-added service for their end users: a less expensive and more reliable than a taxi. They innovate as fast as they can, even though it will eventually demonetize their own business. It's likely they know the future will possibly be without monetary exchange for goods and services, but that's in the future and not today.

Today, there's still lots of money to be made—especially in real estate. That same opportunity may not be there tomorrow.

Cheaper, high-quality services is the operating position of Uber, which arguably may not be at the core value of your real estate brand. Not all clients are created equal: some want a cheaper real estate service, and others will continue to prefer a personal touch and human interaction.

- Are you crystal clear on what values your brand provides to your target niche?

- Do they want cheap and fast or custom and highly-personalized?

- Do you have a clearly-defined demographics and a psychographic profile of your narrow-niched ideal client?

These questions will help you shape the types of services that your business will offer and which types of prospects it will target.

Later in the book, while learning more about Artificial Intelligence (AI), you'll review how AI is clearly defined into general AI and narrow AI. The latter is much more skilled at solving the problem of a narrowly-niched ideal client, and therefore offers superlative value and results.

A realtor and a broker can definitely benefit from a narrow AI approach when you use it to take your million-dollar narrow AI idea to elevate you above the general AI real estate competitors.

In Silicon Valley, at the heart of trendy innovations, the idea of a concierge brand is integrated and flourishes. Why? It's because a company that's known for just one thing and doing it better than anyone else has the power to position itself as a celebrity, authority, and expert.

UBER LESSON #5:
Experimentation

Uber has discovered the demand for ridesharing through a rapidly assembled experiment which allowed them to proceed with ridesharing acceleration, implementation, and domination.

Even though Uber's ridesharing AI algorithm is as complex as quantum computing, the "Celebrity Attraction Brand's" targeting doesn't have to be that complex.

The Anatomy of the Ride Sharing Momentum

Roughly 50% of Uber rides in San Francisco are ride shared, and other cities are starting to follow this trend.

As a real estate professional, you need to discover how this will impact real estate and get ahead of the curve before it's too late. Here are some quick facts about why ridesharing is relevant to real estate:

- ✔ It's 90% utilization;

- ✔ Uber's ridesharing program is as complex as the quantum computer;

- ✔ A community benefits from fewer cars on the road by reduced traffic and fewer emissions;

- ✔ Individuals benefit by not driving through rush hour (estimated 15% of waking time spent driving in many cities);

- ✔ A higher utilization of time in the car is more productive—the era of freedom of time is coming. Los Angeles and Sydney drivers spend two weeks of the year driving. New York is five weeks;

- ✔ There are planetary benefits, with two billion cars in the world, there are nearly two billion drivers. Ridesharing is going to disrupt the car manufacturing industry, which is already disrupted by the electric car revolution initiated by Elon Musk. There will be 2.7 million cars driving into NY daily;

- ✔ 10% of under 30-year-olds have already dropped the car (1 out of 2 in the household); and

- ✔ Starting today with 50% ridesharing in San Francisco, can you imagine how quickly this shift will arrive?

What if you could find a way to apply this win-win-win strategy for your real estate brand? Can you come up with an even better strategy?

Who is to Blame for Cheaper Riders?

If the demand for a cheaper ride wasn't there, Uber wouldn't exist. The same is true for real estate: there's a demand for cheaper real estate models. If the demand for cheaper real estate services wasn't there, those services wouldn't exist. Why blame those working in this niche because they're simply responding to demand?

If we want to blame Uber for massively disrupting not only their own business model but also other industries, including real estate, we should stop paying Uber drivers and start campaigning against... ourselves?

We wanted a faster, cheaper ride from the airports and city centers, and in the middle of the night predictability and reliability. Boom! We wanted it, and here it is.

We are progress-driven, and it's up to us to progress gracefully. Progress promises quantum-leap advantages, and we can spend our priceless time and energy resisting and boycotting, or we can evaluate the opportunities and threats, figure out a new game, and start playing that strategy right now.

Technology and innovation would have never come to our living rooms had we not voted them collectively into existence. Supply and demand. Cause and effect.

Before we get into the Second Suburban Sprawl, let's review the first. According to Wikipedia, *"Urban sprawl or suburban sprawl describes the expansion of human populations away from central urban areas into low-density, monofunctional and usually car-dependent communities, in a process called suburbanization."*

The suburban areas are not as highly priced as the city center. As a result, the shifting real estate demand influences the prices in the suburbs to increase, while for those living in the city center, prices go down. How can a realtor or a broker best prepare for the price adjustments to get ahead of the game?

Wikipedia states the following:

> "The density gradient of industrializing cities has tended to follow a specific pattern: the density of the center of the city would rise during urbanization and the population would remain heavily concentrated in the city center with a rapid decline in settlement towards the periphery. Then, with continued economic growth and the expanding networks of public transport, people (particularly the middle class) would then slowly migrate towards the suburbs, gradually softening the population density gradient. This point was generally reached when the city reached a certain stage of economic development. In London, this point was reached in the first half of the 19th century, in Paris toward the end of the century and in New York City at the turn of the 20th."

CHAPTER 7:
FUTURISTIC CONSEQUENCES
OF AUTHONOMOUS VEHICLS (AV)

Democratization

The second Suburban Sprawl is influenced by the expanding networks of transportation such as autonomous vehicles, Vertical Cars, and the overall ridesharing trend.

While we all still enjoy gathering in cultural and shopping clusters (until VR and AR eventually disrupt this also), most of us won't necessarily want to live in the city centers.

Research shows that 30% of jobs are 90 minutes away from workers' homes, and the lower the income of your client, the further away they're living from public transportation.

It's important to realize that taxis drivers don't like driving away from the city center and avoid driving to the suburbs simply because they make more money on short trips. Uber is democratizing this demand-supply discrepancy for the benefit of the lower income population by enforcing the policy of "reliable ride to anywhere." That's why Uber drivers don't know the client's destination until they've already picked him up, and it's too late to cancel.

Demonetization

Uber is also demonetizing the industry by offering a "cheaper than ever" ride service.

Ridesharing will drive the cost of Uber down further, adding yet another cost reduction factor of autonomous vehicles. Given hypo effective technology utilization, the high cost of which is diluted by the explosive popularity of Uber spread by users, with the advantage of much cheaper service than a taxi – the cost of Uber was attractively low to tip the old trend in its favor.

With the driver's salary being the major cost of the Uber service, autonomous vehicles will make the cost of using Uber 10 times cheaper than car ownership.

With Americans utilizing a car on average 5-10% of their transportation time, and the car absorbing part of our real estate such as square footage of the garage, this alternative is not without merit.

We are already witnessing families giving up their second car and integrating Uber into their daily lives in San Francisco. In a recent survey of the local under-30 population, 10% said they would give up their car—and with the tipping point of the S-curve—this is just the beginning, and indeed a noteworthy data point to consider.

If most of the cars we own are not utilized 90% of the time, and Uber is cheaper and invariably reliable, why own a car? If the garage square-footage is part of the mortgage, there are arguably other ways to use this underutilized space.

Jobs, Traffic, and Autonomous Vehicles

Another factor affecting the Second Suburban Sprawl is the projection for the disappearing of the rush hour traffic caused by the concentration of city-center jobs. With ridesharing, fewer cars will be driving, and they will be doing so much more efficiently. Plus, vertical takeoff cars will make 200-mile commutes a 10-minute breeze.

Can you see why it is not only possible but also enticing for the city-center population to want to spread out? Additionally, if autonomous vehicle Uber offers hands-free rides, resulting in enhanced productivity and 15% of the transit time to be recaptured, why bother driving your own car?

Imagine a ride where you can work, learn or watch movies instead of driving in hot, condensed traffic. There's speculation that we might even enjoy a Jacuzzi inside autonomous vehicles in the future. Plus, it is cheaper and maintenance-free. Isn't this enticing to at least consider?

It's no wonder car ownership is projected to decline and possibly die by 2025. Think about the impact on the prices of commercial real estate spaces and parking spaces. Perhaps they'll be converted into vertical takeoff vehicle launching pads, or charging stations for electric cars to offset shifting demand. As a corollary, how will the city survive without the parking ticket revenue built into their budgets?

Why Autonomous Vehicles are Safer

Did you know that artificial intelligence (AI) empowered autonomous vehicles (AV) have the potential to save millions of lives from car accidents? That includes 10 million lives of children under 10, who are the most frequent fatalities in car accidents. When autonomous vehicles prove super safe, will it be illegal for humans to drive?

It's even possible that AV will be driving our kids without the need for parents to chauffeur them around, saving thousands of hours and boosting productivity in our society. However, the fact that Mom may want to hang out with her kids instead of drive is another aspect to consider.

The same blessing of free time will be available for the nursing and healthcare professionals. As our society lives longer, this could be an elegant solution for the "freedom of time" component.

Another consideration is the effect on the insurance industry when driving becomes 100% safe. Without the drivers to insure, the impact to that industry would be devastating. In the future, Uber will assume insurance. With their safety record, no one will get rich on the premiums. It will be a sad day for insurance agents, but the safety benefit to humanity will be immense.

VERTICAL Take-off and Landing Vehicles (VTOL)

Another accelerator in the Second Suburban Sprawl is the highly anticipated vertical take-off and landing Vehicles (VTOL) fleet that Uber has cued into for deployment. According to Wikipedia, "A vertical take-off and landing Vehicles (VTOL) aircraft is one that can hover, take off, and land vertically." Historically in New York City, rides like these were taken by helicopter. However, this mode was subsequently outlawed after serious accidents.

Research of the VTOL niche revealed a hidden opportunity blocked only by the historical perception that vertical vehicles were unsafe and noisy. But this isn't grounded in fact. Given the technological advancements in artificial intelligence, safety and noise obstacles are much more easily achieved than a mission to Mars.

According to Uber, with the ridesharing trend, the scaling is achievable, and VTOL could become profitable within 10 years. An Uber white paper states that the production of vertical landing and takeoff vehicles is anticipated within five years, and scale is expected within 10 years. Needless to say, projected VTOL scaling is nothing like the aircraft industry has ever seen before.

The main reason to examine cars is that it models a 10-year strategic planning horizon, which is critical in the era of the double-growth curve of technological acceleration. Chinese Alibaba, with the most aggressive growth worldwide, actually dominates with a 100-year strategic horizon. Long-term positioning might be a novelty for a linear thinking realtor, but it's a bare necessity to not only survive but to get ahead and thrive.

Without VTOL, sadly we all might end up needing help. That's why the time to reinvent ourselves inside-out is now. Not tomorrow, not next week, or next month, or next year. The grand game of vertical takeoff in the age of technological renaissance for which you may have been preparing has begun! If you are ready, able, and willing to game, let's game! And one more thing...

CHAPTER 8:
REALTORS ALERT AND
AUTONOMOUS VECHICLES (AV)

A study sponsored by Intel suggests that autonomous vehicles will create at least $7 trillion dollars of "passenger" economy by 2050, with a value derived from time saved in commutes, the products and services sold to address that additional time, and mobility-as-a-service businesses that will generate about $3 trillion in revenue. These impressive numbers highlight the massive positive impact that autonomous vehicles will have on the economy.

The transformation we see in the transportation sector presents a wealth of business opportunities -- despite the fact that much of the global press coverage focuses on the legal drama and technology races between disruptive start-ups and legacy automakers.

Given the fact that real estate represents about 13% of the National GDP, the massive changes in an economic sector as significant as transportation can't help but affect the jobs within the industry.

According to Google, consumers take a million Uber rides daily, which means up to a million or more drivers rely on Uber income. It's not only Uber drivers who will be affected, but also truck drivers, and there are five million of them in the U.S. alone. How will they pay their mortgages?

Peter Diamandis, the founder of Singularity University, once said: "The fastest way to make a million dollars is to solve a problem of a million people." That's 5 million in just the U.S.

Motivational speaker, Tony Robbins recently said, "If we don't deal with those problems now, they will deal with us."

It's true that real estate and home ownership are truly at the heart of all problems, so we, in the real estate industry, are the ones who must find solutions to help the transition into the age of the technological renaissance.

I don't know why you've decided to read this book, but these reasons are exactly why I've decided to write it. I've realized that it's my purpose to help this transition. What's your purpose? How do you want to change the world and make it a better place? If you do have something in mind, may I encourage and empower you to start now?

Uber Lessons You Can't Afford To Miss

We are dematerializing jobs, demonetizing products and services with aggressively lower prices that may eventually become free, and preparing humanity for Universal Basic Income. The question we should be asking ourselves is: "What are we going to do with our free time?" We all have passions, dreams, and aspirations. Should we start thinking about them today? Perhaps.

The priority, however, is psychological innovation if we want a smoother ride into the future of real estate. Not only for ourselves, but for others. As humans, we make decisions emotionally, not logically, and changes will stir up emotions. What's important to remember is that it is up to us to choose how we want to respond to these changes.

What does this mean? As humans, we're meaning makers. We assign meaning mostly by default, not by deliberate choice. We can assign "bad," "wrong," "illegal," and "immoral" to autonomous vehicles, vertical take-off and landing cars, augmented reality, artificial intelligence, and anything else that seems strange or out-of-place. We can also choose to resist and play the victim of the coming transformation that, indeed on some level, we all co-created as a collective consciousness.

We can also apply wisdom, love, grace, honor, and compassion to the world around us, and harness the most positive, brilliant, breathtaking change the universe has ever seen into our own lives. What feels better? Floating down the stream enjoying the journey? Or fight upstream kicking and screaming, struggling and resisting unnecessarily?

You are the only one who can choose, but remember: there is no miserable journey to a happy ending. There never has been, and never will be. Therefore, decide wisely. Commit. Lead. Grow.

Some of the questions we should be asking ourselves are: What can I do to tap into this rising tide of technological renaissance? How can I become the light guiding humanity into its highest and best future?

The truth is, if you believe in goodness deep in your heart, it is time you step up and start playing the new game of doubling with confidence. Modeling success is not for the sake of others, but for you. What will you do?

Harnessing Ridesharing Momentum into Your Brand Innovation

We've just established that ridesharing momentum has been powerful for Uber celebrity status in the industry. Is it possible that "sharing" is a part of a global trend? Isn't Airbnb a sharing trend? Aren't Facebook and social media a sharing trend?

Is it possible that the driving force behind sharing is the human need for love and connection? It's really the behind-the-scenes awakening of human connection that is the fuel behind a big portion of this progress, isn't it?

Stop and think about it: Have you noticed how more people are transplanting into new places and communities inside and outside of the U.S.? Do you realize how retiring couples are more and more considering moving outside of the U.S., and wanting more home for their money? Are you aware how international buyers are investing in second homes in the U.S. and vice-versa? Have you noticed how global, national, and communal transplanting is accelerating?

Are you aligning your daily, weekly tactics, and most importantly, your long-term strategies with those international, national, and communal transplanting trends? Are you too busy working in your business, not on your business, and missing the most lucrative opportunities?

CHAPTER 9:
TIME FREEDOM, FUTURISTIC
COMMUNICITES AND REAL ESTATE

We've already established how we must be preparing for the inevitable freedom of time without jobs. We've also discussed that we must decide which passion we want to pursue, and start taking steps in its direction. If still unclear, consider how in the nearest future artificial intelligence might advise us on hundreds of choices for creation and collaboration. Such advice might include what and how to create, who else might already be working on it around the globe, which expert is available to participate or contribute, who is passionate and might be interested in joining your project, and who has already done a ton of work that has not been published yet for the general public.

Is it possible that the futuristic communities will be idea, value, and project-driven? Just like Facebook and Google have already started building the live-in communities on the job, and forming around common interests, passions, and values, to spend more time together. Many companies are following their lead.

Did you know that Marriott announced a new type of hotel chain where the living space will be much smaller and the common areas for connecting and sharing much larger? Are they the trendsetter or trend follower?

Harnessing Futuristic Community To Become The Market Leader

Uber is riding the long-term strategic momentum of ridesharing. How can a realtor ride the trend of human connection that will be transforming the single-family neighborhood into even more specific common interest driven mini-cities?

You can start forming those communities right now because it will be your bridge into the future. How can you do that? How about curation of the content that you are passionate about? Maybe not even all the content, but rather a more narrow-defined idea.

Our experience and education-based values are nothing else but an idea compound. It's a combustion of knowledge. It's a beautiful mosaic of a combination of different colors, lights, sounds, vibrations, and all of it comes from one idea and explodes into another.

Sharing and connecting trends might be inviting us on the journey to curate ideas and form communities of like-minded people.

The content that connects us the most with any niche, and any community with which we want to be associated.

When we talk about moving into and away from the geographically-based community into the idea community, as the idea curator, new leader, or new innovator of humanity, you have infinite choices for what ideas will help you achieve your goals.

They could be interplanetary-exploration ideas if you're passionate about that. I was sitting on the airplane yesterday next to a man obsessed with space. He wouldn't shut up about space. We all should be talking about things with such passion. In doing so, we connect and form a tribe that resonates uniquely with everyone.

Your tribe could be in Italy on Lake Como, in the South of France in Nice, in India by Taj My Hall... you name it. Obviously for real estate purposes, we want to target a more geographic-based audience, but not always. With the virtual reality and augmented reality explosion, we might start selling virtual real estate!

Examples of Idea-Curated Communicities

How about longevity? If you can't stop thinking and talking about longevity, why not think and talk about it on-point and as a benefit to your business? You might even narrow your focus into rejuvenation and the body's amazing ability to restore itself.

Now that we can print with molecular-atomic precision, can we possibly start preparing for 3D-printed bodies? If we can 3D-print human organs, how long before we can print bodies, or at least restore them to live for 900 years like we used to long ago. Will we be able to 3D-print DNA? The truth is, if we don't start asking these questions, we'll never find out.

You may also be interested in 3D-printed manufacturing, instead of longevity. You may enjoy learning about the green materials that are becoming more available to build new communal housing for your tribe. Chances are there are others who might also be passionate about this, but they are currently sitting alone in the privacy of their home.

Why not start connecting these people into a joyful, rowdy bunch; talking and collaborating together? Make it your community. You might be waiting for something to happen, and so are they. Haven't you waited long enough?

These people will gravitate towards you naturally. You'll attract them. All you need to do is to stand up as a leader with that bright idea, and they'll find you. They'll listen and welcome you. Why? It's because they too can feel the upcoming rapid change in the air, and they too want to connect because they want more security and certainty from you.

When you step up as an idea curator for your tribe, you'll spark their certainty as well as imagination, along with their hope and trust that the technological renaissance is a good thing.

As the future unfolds, we might even start time traveling into the future and the past. Would that be fascinating to talk about? I am not suggesting it's happening today. I'm simply expanding your horizon of what is possible so that you don't restrict yourself from your past experiences, but rather evolve yourself into all that you can be.

SECTION THREE:
AUGMENTED REALITY (AR)
AND THE FUTURE
OF REAL ESTATE AGENTS

CHAPTER 10:
THE RISING TIDE
OF AUGMENTED REALITY

Not all trends are created equal

Some are ripe and potent, while others a waste your time, energy, and money. Virtual Reality (VR) technology is great for both e-Realtors and buyers, and there are many options available for immediate use. Augmented Reality (AR) is just about to burst into user interface adoption, and it will be practical, effective, and profitable. AR represents four times the revenue potential of VR; so if you think VR could give you a competitive advantage in real estate, try AR, which will beat it by four times!

While we think of these as futuristic technologies, both have been developed for over 100 years, and they are now gradually moving into our homes.

Going back to our conversation about an old fashion realtor who will take 20 linear steps and will get 20 linear results, exponential-thinking realtors have already jumped onboard of the fast-speed VR train. Most likely, they are already experimenting with AR. Do not wait for them to pass you by or leave you behind, get started with this technology as soon as possible!

You might be familiar with the company MATTERPOR. COM, which, according to their website, is "the only all-in-one reality capture system that gives you realistic, interactive 3D and VR experiences that feel as real as being there." Concierge VR companies for real estate are also available in most states if you prefer working with the local providers or want a highly-customized experience.

The stream of money flowing into VR and AR combined have a projected $120 billion revenue by 2020 with three-quarters allocated to Augmented Reality.

Experts believe that both VR and AR are going to fundamentally change how we do everything, including communicating, educating, engineering, training, building, buying, selling, and printing. It will also have a profound impact on real estate.

It's generally a good practice to know where billionaires are investing their money. We don't have a billion-dollar R&D department that reports to us every Monday with an updated forecast of the leading industry, but Microsoft and Apple do. We can follow their lead to increase our chances of success.

When you learn that the CEO of Microsoft, Satya Nadella said, *"I believe that every walk of life and every human activity which today is mediated on computers will be transformed by AR,"* you too may decide to pay attention and open your cognitive perception filter to search and locate opportunities that will allow you to harness that trend.

The CEO of Apple, Tim Cook, concurred, saying "there is a virtual reality and there is augmented reality, both of these are incredibly interesting, but my own view is that augmented reality is the larger of the two, probably by far." Some of you might need more proof, but based on my MBA analysis, when both Microsoft and Apple are on board with billions of dollars on the line, it's a solid investment.

The First Self-Contained Augmented Reality (AR) Computer

If you're not convinced you should buy this technology today, let's look more closely at Microsoft HoloLens, an AR leader. I recently attended an AR panel discussion curated by Alex Kipman, the exponential thinker behind Microsoft AR, who answered questions for two hours.

Major AR companies, including ODG, Meta, and Magic Leak, have been leading the race to grab consumers, but the first fully self-contained holographic computer HoloLens was designed by Microsoft.

The Microsoft HoloLens is a headset that will be used with Windows Holographic to see and interact with 3D images, allowing the user to visualize the world holographically.

1. HoloLens self-contained computer-headset has no connection to a cell phone or a computer and works in any location without setup. You just put it on and start seeing holograms in the real world with an incredible level of precision, indistinguishable from real time. This is like Robert Downey Jr. as Tony Stark in the movie "Iron Man" displaying research images in the air.

2. Experts believe that the cell phone is eventually going to disappear into a pair of AR glasses that we are

going to wear, possibly 24/7. Those glasses are going to be our communications tool – our eyes, our ears, and our senses!

3. HoloLens includes the sensors that are detecting your emotions and hand movements and creates a brand new interaction with a computational system indistinguishable from real time. It allows for visualizing massive amounts of data in the context of the real world.

4. Eventually, AR will be able to take all of the Artificial Intelligence information, which ultimately will live in the scalable cloud. This will allow the user to visualize that data, anchored in the real world.

5. AR approaches human perception, which in the real world comes in two dimensions like anything in physics. The universal AR platform will be mostly coming from Microsoft, Apple, Google, and Amazon.

6. The best and most affordable AR devices are starting at $29 from HP, Dell, Lenovo, Acer, and Asus as accessories for PCs. They are not self-contained, but they do offer the highest resolution and the ability to work with no setup.

Challenges

In spite of all this, there are at this point challenges to be overcome.

Comfort

The first challenge of AR is comfort, mostly related to weight. The weight ranges from 60 grams to 600 grams, while a normal pair of glasses is less than 10 grams. Weight makes AR devices uncomfortable to be worn all day. Most people find HoloLens comfortable for about 45 minutes.

Immersion

The second challenge of AR is immersion: how do we start increasing the level of immersion of these devices? As you increase immersion, you're often adding more hardware and therefore more weight. How can we increase immersion without compromising on comfort?

Price

The third challenge of AR is actually price and affordability. Making it affordable to the masses will be important to implementation.

In spite of any of these challenges, if you are innovative, you will hop on board now and learn about and purchase AR software. You can start by investing $3,000 in HoloLens. If you want a less-expensive investment, consider buying a phone with AR features (these are available within the $600 range).

CHAPTER 11:
100% DIGITIZATION OF REAL ESTATE

I've been talking about how future trends will make entering into the digital world essential if you wish to make money in real estate.

I've also tried to impress upon you the need to embrace a philosophy of freedom of choice if you wish to move forward in this new digital world. You must believe that you are in charge of your life and it's your actions that determine your future.

You might be wondering how to apply all this information to your real estate business. To help, we'll start by talking about the basics.

4 Real Estate Buying PHASES

1. Aspirational Phase: Investigate Prices & Home Types; Mild Focus

In this phase, the client is getting curious about the idea of purchasing. The phase lasts 12 to 18 months and over this period of time, they might have sent you an inquiry that asks you about what's available. They're looking into the experience of owning, slowly convincing themselves of the idea of purchasing.

2. Research Phase: Mortgage/Credit/Payments – Narrow Down Areas & Prices; Moderate Focus

For another three to six months, give or take, the client

will enter into the research phase. They will investigate mortgage payments to find out if they can qualify for properties, and will start narrowing the areas that they are looking for according to affordability.

3. Transactional Phase: Focus on Area & Price, Set Appointments, Open Houses; High Urgency

Finally, the prospects will enter the Transactional Phase. At this point, they start booking appointments to view property in person. As a real estate agent, you will show a buyer an average of ten homes over ten weeks.

4. "Under Contract" Phase:

The buyer and seller have made a deal, and the contract is being finalized. During this phase, all interactions are related to the contract, primarily signing the contract and conducting inspections.

100% Digitization of Phases I and II

In both the Aspirational and Research Phase, the real estate buying and selling process has already been greatly empowered and generated digitally. With VR (virtual reality) and AR (augmented reality) adoption by many brokerages, the final phases are becoming digital as well. The real estate process is approaching 100% digitization, with diminishing real-time realtor engagements. Especially with Millennials, texting is gold!

Virtual Reality

Virtual reality is a computer-generated simulation of a three-dimensional environment such as a home. Wearing a headset, the prospective buyer virtually walks through a home without actually being on site. Simple hand or finger motions may even allow you to open doors, explore property amenities, and rearrange furniture.

Augmented Reality

Augmented reality, according to Wikipedia, is "a live direct or indirect view of a physical, real-world environment whose elements are augmented by computer-generated sensory input such as sound, video, graphics or GPS data."

In real estate, augmented reality is being used to bring flat-print materials like blueprints and photos to life, right in front of the client. A real estate professional can pop up a lifelike 3D model of a home that is completely interactive. In the digital replica, the client can modify features such as paint color or try different pieces of furniture, all to scale.

Both VR and AR allow you to take a tour of the house, as the human eye would see it, without actually being there. With software like Rooomy, a virtual staging software, you can even see how the space might look with your choice of decorating.

Digitization of Phases III and IV

The 3rd (Transactional Phase) and the 4th (Under Contract Phase) phase of buying and selling a home is rapidly becoming digital as well.

Transactional Phase is focused on finding the property on

the buyer side and finding the buyer on the seller side. The majority of the activities are heavily based on showing. Traditionally, home showing was real time with real people, but now both VR and AR are fully capable of taking care of this digitally. We're moving to anytime with no people.

The Under Contract Phase is heavily based on executing the contract, including conducting, negotiating, and resolving inspection issues. AR is perfectly capable of taking care of inspection and offering you a "presence" effect at the specific location, even if you or your client are on vacation in Fiji. The benefit being location-free transactions.

We talked about freedom as the primary driving force of human motivation. Digitization in our case through the adoption of VR and AR opens you up to international real estate.

Last but not least, the second element of the 4th Under Contract Phase is actually signing the addendum on multiple negotiating points has all been digitized.

For instance, there is the massive adoption of DocuSign by not only technology-driven real estate brokerages but by the traditionalists. If you're not familiar with DocuSign, it is the digital real estate service that allows any part of the transaction to sign any sections of the real estate contract over a mobile device from anywhere in the world at any time.

CONCLUSIONS:

VR (virtual reality) will allow previewing of the homes from anywhere, anytime either by using the computer or mobile without setting up appointments and coordinating appointment time with a real estate agent.

Once adopted, VR and AR will make the home showing activity of the real estate transaction digital. And it's possible to speculate that the next logical step in the acceleration of digitization could be fully digitized VR and AR home showing as a part of the Research Phase, not the agent-driven Transaction Phase.

As we can see, digitization in real estate is moving along full speed, but... what is the future of the real estate agents?

Winning the Future of Real Estate with Augmented Reality (AR)

The fundaments of the real estate transaction require Realtors and brokers to continuously polish their sales skills. AR dramatically enhances conversion of a digital (online) lead into a nearly-guaranteed closing, just like an experienced car salesman who offers you to test drive the car. Both VR and AR offers give your online lead an opportunity to intimately "see" and "experience" living inside this home. AR takes it to the next level by offering an opportunity for your lead to interact with digital objects in the hologram by moving or removing the furniture and replacing it with your choices of appliances, couches, chairs, and even new paint on the wall. With time, AR will be able to show the whole remodeling process, as they are currently doing with success in the commercial real estate market.

A great company that offers AR for real estate is Rooomey. com, which focuses on interaction with furniture and staging within the room.

There is an amazing case study for AR application in commercial real estate. Greg Lynn, the famous architect, used Microsoft HoloLens and Trimble software to redesign an entire factory in space in Detroit by using AR from the beginning to the end of the construction project. If you are a contractor and want to try AR, all you need to do is to buy HoloLens, download Trimble, and start using it without writing a line of code. You can literally start constructing buildings, parking lots, bridges, cities, and houses faster, easier, and with more variety, and you can do it all instantly!

By engaging your client to actively and viscerally interact with the environment of the future home itself, you are literally letting your client "test drive" living in this home and getting them emotionally involved. Also, those clients who might have been wasting your time driving around from house to house are now ready to buy. It's likely that AR will expedite the process of previewing the homes because their emotional taste buttons are on fire and they can't wait to start living in the new house. With all these enhancements, it's possible to free enough of your time to work more on your business not in the business, which always leads to more income.

AR enhanced processes of buying and selling homes are rooted in the psychology of sales, which states that 90% of your client decisions are made with emotions, only 10% are made through logic, and most of the time, this logic is simply used to justify emotions. Do you see how digital real estate can shorten the buying process and bring higher quality experience into it?

There is not much difference between VR and AR, it is just a matter of the degree of density between environments, objects, and people. VR and AR are navigating the different worlds of digits and objects; worlds that are beginning to interact with each other.

AR and VR serve as a bridge between our current reality and digital reality, allowing the two to merge, play, interact, and co-create. With time the digital world will become more real and what we see will become more digital, even though those two parallel universes existed in two different dimensions.

That means that we're going to experience digital objects falling off the computer and into our "reality." We're going to experience people teleporting into different times and spaces. We're going to experience information in a very, very different way.

> "With the advent of sensors, with the advent of artificial intelligence and the advent of the computer, for the first time ever we are able to intercept these two universes and mix realities that try to define the intersection between the analog and the digital, between atoms and bits, between what is real and what is virtual by essentially merging the positives of both universes. The fact that it is immersive, the fact that it is connected in real time while maintaining the ability for us as humans to now have the super power to displace space and time."

> - Alex Kipman, Microsoft HoloLens co-inventor, who has his name on 150 patterns.

CHAPTER 12:
"THE FUTURE OF THE REAL ESTATE"
BUSINESS MODEL

At this point some of you might be worrying that technology could eliminate the need for a real estate agent and broker altogether. Fortunately, this is not likely to happen.

There was a time when real estate agents were the secret keepers of properties. Since then, the value-add of the agents has shifted. Yet, what remained is the trusted evaluation that agents continue to provide every day.

When buyers enter the Transactional Phase of purchasing the home, they are researching not only the property but also the real estate agent. They need to they can trust you to help them make the biggest investment decision in their life.

Real Estate clients want the neighborhood, home, and process-insights that, so far, a computer cannot provide. People buy from people they know, like, and trust, and it's only the agent who can provide all three through human face to face interaction.

Even home price evaluation that seems logical and predictable is hard to provide digitally, largely because not every home is created equal. That's why an appraisal is always done by a human and none of the mortgages could be issued without an appraisal conducted by a professional, not a program.

My personal journey started with buying 20 properties in eighteen months before I became a licensed real estate agent, so I understand that every transaction is a masterpiece.

There are human emotions that AI will have difficulty duplicating. It will also have trouble with intuition. I remember selling a home to a friend (which is the hardest thing to do by the way) and walking into a home knowing that it was the right home for my friend, even though she didn't think so.

When I shared my intuitive insights with her, she didn't agree though we always had maintained a rapport. Two weeks later, she realized that the house I pointed out to her was "the one." Luckily, the other offer that was already in place fell through and we did get the house, where, I am proud to say, she still happily resides eight years later!

I used to tell my short-sale seller, "Now that you've hired me, you can stop worrying, because I will worry for you. And when the time comes to worry, I will let you know."

The sigh of relief and the look on their face always told me that they've understood me clearly, and things almost always worked out just fine.

Instances like that are more like a rule rather than an exception and, digital or not, technology won't ever be able to replace the real estate broker. But if you don't do it right, the aggressive capture of market share by the technology-driven real estate companies will occur.

With the increasing pressure from technology, we will be forced to be our absolute best if we wish to realize our dreams.

The question you should be asking yourself now is:

Am I in the right industry?

Because if you are not, today is a good opportunity to start looking around for the passion and purpose that we all have within.

And it's time we unleash our power.

It's time for us to adopt AR technology to enhance what we are already doing well. What are the general aspects of AR that are making this technology a must-have in our real estate arsenal?

CHAPTER 13:
9 STEPS TO WINNING
LEADS GENERATION

For many new Realtors, lead generation is the most important part of their business. They assume that if they can gather a large list of leads, they will inevitably be successful.

But experienced Realtors know that it's not lead generation that counts, but lead conversion.

With modern technology, you can easily find leads in just a few minutes. Everyone who calls themselves a realtor has access to hundreds or even thousands of leads. Using the technology properly, however, can put you above the competition and make you one of the most successful realtors in your area.

You either use technology effectively, or you fail. It's that simple.

And it all starts with taking the right steps towards lead generation...

1. Create a Pipeline of Quality Leads

Having a pipeline of leads is not enough. You need to start with a source of quality leads. This can take experimenting and trial-and-error, but you should utilize both traditional and creative technologies, websites, and social media to create high-quality leads.

You should use Facebook, Broker.com, Trulia, and Zillow, as well as other sources. With quality leads that are actually in the market to buy – not casual "lookers" who waste everyone's time — you can start focusing on clients that will help boost your income.

2. Automate Your Responses

In many cases, people looking for a Realtor will go with the first agent that contacts them. This means you need to be swift with your messages and respond to leads as quickly as possible before someone else comes in and snatches away your business.

Automation can be an important ally. With automated messaging technology, you can contact new leads almost any time; when you are showing a house, finalizing papers, or relaxing at home.

3. Manage Your Workflow

With the right tools, technology, and systems in place, you'll know exactly what to do and when to do it. At all times, you want to be productive and take steps that are effective; you don't want to be spinning your wheel and getting nowhere.

You want traction; proper workflow management gives you that traction.

4. Nurture Your Clients

There are also tools that help you nurture your clients and guide them through the real estate process. You need to nurture your clients and help them make the right choice, without making them feel pressured or forced.

There are many tools you can utilize to nurture your clients. With a nurturing attitude and the right tools, you can easily turn your leads into dollars.

5. Implement RealScout

RealScout is an effective technology to acquire and track leads. It has excellent features that make the organization of leads more effectively, allowing you to respond to leads, and even reassign leads to different team members.

RealScout has a convenient dashboard that makes tracking and managing leads simple. There is even a tool that allows buyers to schedule a showing, thus making it easier for you to meet and interact with clients.

6. Send Texts with Riley

Riley is one of the biggest tools for converting leads and enhancing your real estate business. This platform is a 24-hour texting platform that uses live human beings to create personalized, reliable customer contact. They can contact all of your leads and they work off a time-tested script that is extremely effective.

They also guarantee a two-minute response time, which means your customers are contacted quickly, making them feel appreciated, which is the start of a nurturing, quality realtor-client relationship.

7. Use Chime for Your CRM

Managing your client relationships is vital, and Chime is one of the most respected platforms for CRM in the real estate industry. They have a cost-effective platform, a mobile app, lead routing, and lead broadcasting, which ensures no lead is wasted.

The desktop for Chime is also simple and easy to use. It shows contact information and provides a communication history between you and the client.

8. MailChimp

Staying in touch with your clients is essential in achieving top-quality lead conversion stats. MailChimp can help you send emails to a single or multiple clients, keeping you and your real estate team top of mind with the customer.

MailChimp has many different features that allow you to tailor your messages to fit your business and your customers, creating more effective interactions and enhancing lead conversions.

9. Educate Your Clients

As a final step, we'd like to remind you to educate your clients throughout the entire process. Many people, especially young first-time homebuyers, are not certain about the real estate process and don't know what to expect from their Realtor.

You should educate clients about the real estate process, giving them information about inspections, closings, mortgages, appraisals, and more. You can work this information into MailChimp messages, Riley texts, and interactions through RealScout.

Final Take Aways from Lead Conversion:

Tip #1: Use Lead Generation Best Practices for Technology

Remember to use the top technology and software to have the best results for your efforts. Use Realtor, Zillow, and other effective sites, and always stay up to date on the best practices.

Tip #2: Lead Conversion Best Practices Recommendations

Use Riley, MailChimp, and RealScout effectively and make sure to do it frequently and fast. If you're not on these programs, get on board NOW!

SECTION FOUR:
ARTIFICIAL INTELLIGENCE (AI)
& THE FUTURE
OF THE REAL ESTATE AGENTS

CHAPTER 14:
THE MIRACLE AND THE PROMISE
OF ARTIFICIAL INTELLIGENCE (AI)
IN REAL ESTATE.

"AI is not just a game changing technology, it's totally disrupting the entire playing field that all of you are operating on."

— Neil Jacobstein, IMB Watson

Recent advances in Artificial Intelligence (AI) are truly remarkable, and quite frankly, bordering on science fiction, except that they are real. And they are happening right now. Some of these advances have profound implications on how everything in the future will work, including residential real estate. Specifically these AI advances will determine how buyers, sellers, and agents interact with each other, and with the property they are buying or selling.

First, let's look at how AI works and how it has evolved into "thinking machines." Today, AI computers can replicate some of the most complicated human intellectual processes, those which separate us from all other things on this planet. For example, research scientists are building AI computer programs that process information in the way humans do. These AI machines, like the human brain, observe things around them, process that information, and calculate what action is best for achieving a particular goal or objective. It often accomplishes this over time through trial and error, just like people do. It is programmed to "learn" from its past experiences. In other words, the computer has an algorithm that gathers and stores past information, which helps it make better choices in the future based on past experiences. This is exactly how the human thought process works, and it's pretty scary to think a machine can do this.

"It Feels Right" Artificial Intelligence (AI)

In fact, in many respects, some machines can think better than humans. Several years ago, IBM built a computer called Deep Blue, which was programmed to play chess. Deep Blue's program was filled with all the possible moves on the chess board. It was also given the games of past champions so it could understand what moves brought it closer to the objective of winning. After years of refinement and algorithmic learning, Deep Blue beat the world's top ranked chess players.

Believe it or not, chess isn't the toughest game for AI machines to play. There's one called GO, an ancient Chinese game, popular among over 40 million players today, that is even harder to master. The number of possible moves in chess, are 32 per move vs. 200 per move with GO. Importantly, top players of GO claim they rely more on creativity and intuition – "it just feels right" – as compared to champion chess players who claim their moves are based more often on logic.

A new AI program was created to model the intellectual behavior of top GO players and to actually come up with uniquely human-type original thought that would help the program beat champion GO players. In other words, this AI machine would "think" like people do, coming up with moves that did not exist before. By being creative, this AI program could beat the best.

Sure enough, this new AI machine beat the number one GO player in the world and did so, in part, by developing some entirely new strategies and tactics. The machine was creating original thought!

Elon Musk, the head of Tesla, and founder of PayPal, among others, raised a stark warning recently about how AI, if not properly controlled, could pose a threat to human civilization. He and others have said AI technology could spin out of control and learn behavior that is dangerous and not anticipated by programmers. An AI machine might, for example, in its quest to achieve a certain objective, work out a way that would prevent humans from turning the machine off. Who knows to what extent the machine would go to reach its programmed goal?

Some might consider it scary, but there is another perspective. The rising tide of AI might prove an exciting challenge and an invitation for humans to step up to bigger game of realizing more of our latent potential.

On the safety first site, researchers at Stanford University and U.C. Berkeley are working on programs that would prevent AI machines from going "rouge" and performing actions that are detrimental to people. Nobody wants a bunch of machines out-thinking humans and ruling the world. This may sound like science fiction, but it's about to become real. Why would they do that? Given the history of humans going "rouge" on a few occasions, we want to land on the safe side of evolution of artificial intelligence.

Putting Sci-Fi fear scenarios aside, there are many benefits that AI brings to society. It will, at the very least, make everything more many times over more efficient and productive. Advances in medical research are only now starting to benefit from AI. Pretty soon AI technology will be driving our cars, flying military aircraft and performing all sorts of functions that people used to do. This, hopefully, will free mankind up in the nearest future from the more mundane tasks of everyday life, and allow people to pursue more fulfilling lives. And that is the promise that is worth our awareness because it is aligned with the desire for expansion into the future of our dreams individually and collectively.

AI Awakening and the Future of the Real Estate Agents

But how, exactly, will this AI revolution impact the real estate agents? Will it replace them?

Some fear that AI could eventually replace agents and brokers. The thinking is that AI machines will become so smart that they will be able to do all the functions now handled by human real estate agents. I wouldn't worry about that yet, but we all know the effect of self-fulfilling proficiencies and the consequences of choices, especially complacency.

Ever since the Internet came on the scene, people have said that real estate agents were headed for extinction.

The Web, it was said, would disintermediate agents and brokers. Who needs them when everything can be done online by machines that are smarter than people, and cheaper to operate?

Hundreds of millions of dollars in venture capital has been spent on startup models that were going to achieve that goal. Today, the graveyard of "new real estate models" is littered with tech startups that tried, and failed to remove the human element from real estate transactions. There are, right now, a number of broker models that are trying to automate the real estate transaction process entirely. These are likely to fail too because home buyers and sellers want a person beside them, not a machine when they embark on the most significant financial transaction of their lives. AI machines might and will enhance the experience in ways that we can't even comprehend yet, but they will never replace a human connection fueled by our innate desire for understanding, compassion, and empathy.

Can you imagine an AI robot doing a walk-through with a potential buyer? Not likely or at least not yet, but if you open your filters of perception, you might spot the opportunities of integrating AI into your exponential real estate business model that others are not thinking about. And this is where it can get exciting for you, your clients, and your commissions.

AI technology will impact everything and real estate will be no exception, and it can benefit brokers and agents who take advantage of it. This technology will allow buyers, sellers, and agents to make smarter decisions, faster. For example, property searches will be more precise and quicker. Simple real estate tasks could be handled by AI, freeing agents up to pitch more listings or spend more time with clients.

AI will also help with customer outreach. It can lessen the time between a prospect's inquiry and an agent's response. AI programs can also provide a more in-depth picture of people who are, for example, about to list their homes but haven't yet decided with whom to list it with. Data on the demographic and behavioral characteristics of this group will be "learned" by the AI program. It will build a construct of who to target, and when to approach them. AI could create an algorithmically developed script that will greatly increase the success-rate of an agent's new listing presentations.

Pretty much everything we do today can be improved with AI except the flesh and blood connection people have among themselves. AI should not be feared, but embraced. Those who learn to leverage AI will increase their income, and be miles ahead of the pack.

CHAPTER 15:
ARTIFICIAL INTELLIGENCE (AI)
FACT SHEETS

✔ Artificial Intelligence (AI) has an impressive list of the major players, including Google, Amazon, Facebook, IBM, and Microsoft.

✔ Six decades of intense R&D in AI has led to explosive growth, which continues to evolve at an accelerating pace. CB Insights have identified the top 100 startups in the field; most didn't exist just a few years ago.

✔ Investments and deals totaled $589 million across 160 deals in 2012. In 2016, there was over $5 billion in investments and 658 deals.

✔ More than 60 startups are already using deep learning to transform operations from sales and CRM and even security.

✔ The first hedge fund, Numerai, will open this summer, on the order of an expected $100 million. The future of investing is going to be a lot of AI-driven moves. This will be the first massively machine-learning, data-scientist driven hedge fund.

✔ Doctors can diagnose pulmonary hypertension and predict which patients will die with about 60% accuracy.

✔ In January 2017, a Northwestern professor announced that his team created an AI that outperformed the average American on intelligence testing, scoring in the 70th percentile.

✔ In October 2015, AlphaGo, a program developed to play the board game Go, became the first program to beat a professional Go player without handicaps on a full-sized 19×19 board. In 2016, a mysterious player named Master, ripped through the championship China community before it was revealed that the player was actually AlphaGo.

General AI and Narrow AI

General AI and narrow AI.... if AI develops through niches, shouldn't we?

The most brilliant minds are thinking that AI is not going to hit us all at once. Instead, it's going to be a gradual transition from general AI to neuro AI.

General AI deals with systems and generalizations, including specific niches like learning to play chess.

What's going to happen with all those start-ups? They will pick niches; the convergent niches between Artificial Intelligence and Augmented Realities? Will they choose between CRM and sales, between colleges, education, medicine, and training?

They'll pick a niche and create an AI like neuro AI. In a thousand year, the whole real world will be covered with those neuro AIs that are specialized and integrated into our lives. It will probably be governed by the general AI or through the cloud.

AI Applications

AI can be applied across all of these areas, such as design, diagnosis, and manufacturing, as well as management, customer service, sales, configuration, and quality control.

A study of over 360 applications of AI showed that it's not just better, it's also different. AI allows us to expand the range of possibilities, to do things that we couldn't do before.

AI might be a good idea in the near future because Amazon's ECO was the number one Christmas gift this year! Amazon's Echo and Dot turned out to be the top gifts at Amazon, and for good reason. When Echo was first introduced in September of 2015, it had 14 skills. By June of 2016, 1,000 skills. Just seven months later, it had 7,000 skills!

Develop Critical Expertise with AI

Investing in AI is a low-risk opportunity, giving you the chance to double and triple your income and become an authority by developing a critical expertise. Digitizing and dematerializing will lead to you freeing more time to work on the business; not in the business.

There's no reason to reinvent the wheel; others are already modeling adoptions, and all you need to do is find your next step and join!

Google's neuro-translation machine is now able to produce a zero-shock translation. This system gives language translation, and without any additional training, you can now do Korean to Japanese and Japanese to Korean; that's an amazing result!

The dissolution of the language barrier will affect the opening and closing of niches. If U.S. real estate leaders will not start expanding into international markets, international real estate experts will expand into the U.S., redistributing influence and power.

The potential for AI is only limited by our imagination. Imagine AI with a chip that watches your email activity and then creates your email campaign with a specific behavior and writing style designed for each contact. If your contact is auditory, AI will use an auditory writing style; if the contact prefers visual, then AI will adjust your message and pick a different headline. It could also choose a new topic depending on factors, including date or time. Can you imagine the deep trust you will have with clients because of the AI?

CHAPTER 16:
THE FUTURE WORLD
OF ARTIFICIAL INTELLIGENCE (AI)

We are constantly going through deletions, distortions, and generalization of information. AI doesn't have this problem, accessing equally unbiased data and all the facts without discrimination or emotion.

All those possibilities and opportunities are available to us right here, right now because of the machine-learning AI.

Imagine waking up in the morning and having AI give you the exact music you want at the precise volume you prefer. Wouldn't it be paradise?

What about human behavior?

When unbiased information is unblocked and we have full access to algorithms that are embedded in a variety of different devices, eventually those devices will disappear into a tiny chip that can be placed in the brain for intellectual super powers, all connected to a universal bank of knowledge.

Imagine having access to what Bill Gates is thinking! What if we could learn directly from geniuses in the past? We can equally apply the same process to access the wisdom and technologies of the future!

Evolution In A Box Called "NANO"

What if AI could make suggestions for different behaviors? What if it could suggest wake up times depending on a virtual blood test?

Are you beginning to feel like we're getting this evolution in a box, which is more like a Nano chip revolution?

It took humanity ages to evolve from one stage to another, from one moral standard to another, from rural to industrial to the computer and now AI, AR, AV, and more. Up until now, we've been learning through trial and error and slowly evolving through lifetime lessons. Yet now, AI could tap into so many more resources to determine your deepest likes, fears, ideals, and values as well as patterns of behavior and tell you up front the chances of something working. You will still make a choice, but you are much more informed and intelligent about your choices.

The same with business partners, and the best vocation for each person individually, which may or may not be real estate. And now we'll have time and resources to explore and realize that potential.

How amazing it would be to have AI advise us on the most important life choices, but also the best path for today's work. Have you ever been curious about why you are super productive one day and unproductive the next? What if that was no longer the case? How much more productive and fulfilled would we all be?

AI could suggest if you should take certain clients, and save you important time. It could tell you whether to open a business in a new location or deepen your current market.

It took all of us so many experiences to figure who we are. With the help of AI, we will never raise our voice at our partner or child because you will know exactly why they do things in certain ways.

And the more we advance and prosper with our clients, business, community, and family, the more machine-learning is going on and improving.

COMMUNITY SHARING & OPTIMIZING RESOURCES

Imagine the level of humanity that would be interacting within your family and the community. Utilization will go up, and then we're going to start moving from human needs up the hierarchy into wants....

The ERA of Wants and... Freedom

Are you beginning to realize how, with heightened productivity, we're going to start moving to the era of wants?

The main contributor is AI with its ability to synthesize deep-learning algorithms and unbiased data into superior, easier, and faster results.

Could we be excited about learning instantly all those things we've always wanted to know and integrating them into a natural way of being and then learning more?

Wouldn't it be amazing if you could get all those benefits of super foods with the instant fresh-squeezed juices done for you like they do in Malaysia? Imagine eating a dessert that tastes like a desert, but has all the qualities of a healthy salad?

And then AR will show us how our body, mind, and spirit will look like with all those habits in place ten years from now. Then we will not only see but experience how it would feel to live in the future or in the past.

We can start drawing our dream businesses, clients, transactions, and income, then put VR goggles on and experience them in real time. Then we can see from the future backward and know exactly what steps we have taken to achieve such amazing results!

With such mixing and matching, doubling and tripling our income can be effortless. Adding a physiological anchor would accelerate our results. Our motivation will go through the roof and our behavior will change...so will the results!

The only question on our minds will be the first-world question: "What do I want right now?"

Does it feel like all the problems will automatically fall apart, and we're going to start developing new neurological paths that we've always wanted but never felt that we could?

PERSONAL EVOLUTION (DESIRED STATE) IN MINUTES:

The personal transformation is developing in minutes, and the learning curve is closing in on zero. We are beginning to move into the era of synchronicities. In the past, we would say, "If I had a magic wand." Today we'd say, "If I had an AI."

With it, we bypass negative behavior, limiting beliefs, and start being the best of who we truly are.

We are currently "married" to our cell phones. Maybe it's logical that we will be equally attached to our AI programs.

It's not only an individual phenomenon. The same goes for community, regional, national, and global advisors who are allocating resources to fight hunger.

Can you imagine what kind of life we will all be living if we integrate AI? It truly feels, looks, and sounds like the promise of the golden age of abundance and the highest and best ideals of caring, loving, and sharing.

IF THIS IS NOT FREEDOM, WHAT IS?

CHAPTER 17:
9 STEPS TO GET STARTED
WITH AI AND DIGITIZE
YOUR REAL ESTATE BUSINESS

It's not enough to adopt a change, you have to implement it with energy and enthusiasm!

When implementing AI and digitization into your real estate business, you need to create a plan, get buy-in from agents, and employ the plan with vibrant, relentless energy.

Investing in software can be an important part of your path to real estate success, so use these nine tips and you'll have a plan that works for you, your agents, and your budget...

Throw All Your Office Papers in the Trash

This is kind of your jump-off-the-diving-board moment when implementing AI and digitization in your real estate company. A more accurate (and scary) analogy might be burning the ships because there should be no turning back. Throwing papers in the trash is what ERA Evergreen broker Michael Gonzalez did when he started his efforts in 2011.

It was a big step, but this measure freed him from clutter while forcing him to pursue digitization.

Adopt Technology You Can Integrate with Current Tools

Your team has many different tools that they are currently using, so the best AI and digitization strategy works with all the different devices and programs you currently have. With this strategy, you'll be better equipped to adopt technology that makes you more efficient.

It can also make the adoption more affordable, as you won't be forced to spend money on new devices and programs.

Move to a Single Platform with DocuSign Transaction Rooms

Many real estate professionals, including Gonzalez, say that the efficiencies and performance of DocuSign Transaction Rooms are incredible. It has excellent mobile and data storage, and agents in the field can call about a specific transaction at any time.

Agents can contact company leaders about certain issues and the information can be pulled up quickly. If your agency were to get audited, the information needed would be available almost instantly, significantly reducing the hassle and the potential harm to business operations.

Set Lofty Goals and Aspirations

Setting the bar high is okay. In many cases, it will help you stay above the competition. Jimmy Dunlin, the owner of Re/Max Ability Plus in Indiana, set huge expectations for his digitization and AI implementation. In fact, he set the bar at $1 billion in transactions per year!

That's a huge goal, but the lofty expectations kept him driving forward, finding ways to use technology to better enhance his real estate operation. He used the intranet, accounting packages, and other programs to reach his goals.

Make Sure Everyone is Using the Same Platform

One of the challenges you will have in your real estate business is connectivity. Although various programs and devices are becoming more compatible, there are still differences. With different players in different areas, it's important to find company-wide processes that link together.

With DocuSign Transaction Rooms and API integration, you can eliminate many of the roadblocks faced by your office. In the end, this will mean greater communication and efficiencies.

Train Thoroughly

Without proper implementation, your digitization and AI efforts are bound to fail. One of the most important elements of implementation is training. Systems like DocuSign provide training to brokerage firms, going as far as sending trainers to offices for smooth adoption.

Remember that training on any platform never ends because modern platforms never stay the same.

Tailor Training to Groups of Agents

Even the best training program needs to be versatile, nimble, and adaptable. Some agents will not be as accustomed to the specific platforms or programs in general, so you may need to adjust training to fit the specific needs of individuals or larger groups.

By adjusting training to each agent, you'll increase the chances of buy-in from agents, which will result in better operations from start to finish.

Discourage Stubbornness Lightly

Although using the term "mandatory" may not be necessary, you'll want to make it abundantly clear that this digitization and AI implementation is expected from all real estate agents and professionals in your organization. If needed, you may need to require that agents who still prefer paper methods to pay for the processing fees themselves.

The best path, however, is to outline the advantages of AI, so you have informed agents who genuinely want to use the new system.

Pick a Path and Stick to It

From the very beginning, you need to choose your path and stick to it. When implementing AI and digitization, you can't bounce from one strategy and software to another; you need to be clear, steady, and prepared, then stick to the plan.

When you implement the plan with energy and enthusiasm, you'll have a staff of agents who want to increase your success and a list of clients that want to send you their money!

CHAPTER 18:
9 WAYS ARTIFICIAL INTELLIGENCE (AI) IS USED IN REAL ESTATE

AI is changing the world, and real estate is certainly not immune to these changes. Nor would it want to be! Real estate agents need to understand that using AI and other technologies is no longer an option, it's an absolute must.

And the first step, like any game-changing technology, is to understand how AI is being used in real estate.

Targeted Content

Using dynamic information based on a user's submitted data and activity, you can create real estate content for subscribers based on various factors like property choices, areas, income levels, purchasing habits, and more.

Using information and the assistance of artificial intelligence, you can create customized content that speaks to the specific interests and preferences of certain home buyers or sellers. Thanks to AI, the content you send can be based on personalized factors, not a one-size-fits-all message. Without AI, sending these types of tailored messages would be time-consuming and nearly impossible.

Machine Learning from Search Engines

What if search engines could learn from past queries and clicks and deliver results that best suit your profile? That's pretty much what the major search engines are doing now, and it's starting to be used in the real estate business.

Search engines that use machine learning are able to cut through the indefinable aspects of a house that make it someone's dream home, creating a better search experience that is more enjoyable for users and effective for real estate professionals.

Advanced Filter

When a company has a database of houses, users can filter the listings to narrow down results, bringing items that fit their specific area or budget, for example. With advanced filters that are influenced by artificial intelligence, more useful and detailed filters can be created.

For example, users may be able to search through houses with front porches, decks, views of water, and other factors that some people find important.

Image Recognition

When you search Google images for, say, a German shepherd, the results are currently based on the wording and tags used in and around those pictures. Only images that are surrounded by the word "German shepherd" appear. If the picture is a boat, but someone tagged it with "German shepherd," it would still show up on your search.

However, technology is being developed that allows programs to scan a picture and automatically know what it is, regardless of the text. This will be used extensively in real estate to describe and even categorize images to give better information. This will also eliminate the need for manual entry of information, saving real estate professionals' valuable time.

Property Suggestions

Imagine if you could automatically send suggestions for properties based on a client's information? With real estate AI technology, that's becoming a reality. A recent competition between a broker and a bot sent real estate suggestions to a buyer for three days in a row. All three days, the buyer preferred the bot's suggestions over the brokers.

What's more, the buyer was unable to tell which suggestions came from the human and which came from AI. So not only did the buyer prefer the bot's suggestions, he couldn't tell that it was a bot at all!

Chatbots

Certain questions will inevitably require a human answer, but there are many questions that can be handled by a chatbot driven by artificial intelligence. Chatbots can give answers to questions that are based on simple facts like price, features, and building dates. As the technology becomes more sophisticated, the bots will be able to answer more and more complex questions.

This will help real estate agents to juggle multiple questions at once and enhance the buyer experience. Because agents spend less time answering questions, AI also helps them take on more clients, which inevitably leads to more closings!

Document Scanning

There are lots and lots of documents in real estate. There are scanned documents for leases and titles, as well as information documents on home and the buying process. When these documents are scanned, you basically have an image of the document, not a workable format like a Word document.

With document scanning technology, programs can read an image and automatically turn it into a usable, editable document. This once again reduces time, but more significantly, it reduces the chances for mistakes such as lost data or missing information.

Playing Matchmaker for Buyers and Sellers

Just turn on your television and you'll find plenty of commercials for websites that match people looking for romance. There are now similar AI algorithms that play matchmaker for the real estate industry, connecting buyers, sellers, agents, mortgage brokers, and more.

By connecting the right people quickly, the real estate universe becomes more efficient and more welcoming to everyone!

Prepare a Home for Showings

There is one last trick that AI can perform in the real estate industry. It can help prepare a home for a showing! With connected homes, which will become more common throughout the coming decades, connected agents can turn on lights, adjust temperatures, play music, and even activate cleaning bots.

When potential buyers tour the house, they'll find a fully-prepared home, even if the agent just arrived!

SECTION FIVE:
THE FUTURE
OF REAL ESTATE MARKETING

CHAPTER 19:
THE EXPONENTIAL REALTOR MINDSET

Is the Universe A Friendly Place?

I recently posted a question that Einstein considered significant: "The most important question you can ever ask is if the universe is a friendly place?" This post elicited more than 60 comments and the majority of answers stated "yes."

If we believe in a friendly universe, we must believe in owning our personal power that directly affects our ability to choose, create, and live the consequences. We define in what reality we want to live individually and collectively by default, but we have the ability to be more deliberate about it. As creators, we are unlimited, but only if we believe.

We create our own reality that provides us with feedback from our efforts. Did the task work well? Congratulations. It turned out not so hot? Learn, adjust, and do it again... but differently. It's an endless cycle to master our reality. At this point, we must harness the power of technology to meet more of our human needs and wants—not the other way around.

Technologies such as AI, AR, or AV are the expression of our collective human desire to live bolder, fuller, more abundant lives. Nothing, including technology, can alter it unless we say otherwise.

The understanding of our freedom to choose, create, and live the consequences individually and collectively is the primary governing principle of existence. There's nothing that resides above it. That's why the fear of AI can become a self-fulfilling prophecy...but why would we reverse human evolution? Fear arises when and if we don't own the consequences of our choices, and, in turn, don't trust ourselves.

So back to the original question of whether the universe is a friendly place.

It's possible that as a collective consciousness with a strong desire for well-being, we've decided to harness AI for our own convenience and efficacy. If we haven't, it wouldn't have worked anyway because any wars or disaster always intensify desire for more well-being long-term.

Sometimes I feel that the Second World War pushed the desire of humanity for well-being over the tipping point, and with it, the momentum of good will overtook complacency, greed, and power struggle. Our collective freedom will impact world events. That means that what you think and do individually counts!

As a result of the collective human experience of the Second World War, our society became more conscious and deliberate about what we focus on. In a way, this influenced the end of Cold War, the fall of the Berlin War, and opened the floodgate of technological renaissance that's now offering us the opportunity to again "reinvent ourselves" individually and collectively. We can now focus on the task of creating abundance and using our awesome powers to ask evolution-provoking questions, think the unthinkable, and create what has yet to be created—

including doubling our income and inviting others to do the same. And we can do it not because technology pressures us to play a bigger bolder game, but perhaps just for the fun of it!

Intellectually, AR, AI, and AV may be superior to our conscious mind's ability to process a vast amount of information. However, our individual and collective free will is still a powerful force to behold. We should start using this power now to achieve unthinkable results.

Finally, a word of warning: Never underestimate what one individual who owns his or her power and acts can do. Look at Elon Musk...we all have an Elon Musk within us.

Digital Technology vs. Computational Complexity

Interestingly, the machine learning component of artificial intelligence implies that machines are learning from us and then surpassing our conscious minds. However, our conscious mind is just a fraction of who we are, as experts contend that the effect of unconscious and super conscious minds is even more powerful than any AI. Perhaps that's why in the world of technology, humans are often referred to as a computational complexity and believed more valuable than even the brilliance of artificial intelligence.

This begs the question, "Why not combine the best of human intelligence with the best of Artificial Intelligence and live be our happiest and more productive?"

Today I live in America, my second homeland, that offers impressive economic, political, and lifestyle standards when compared to the majority of the world. Today those standards are obsolete and as a result, restrictive, which might explain why innovation and growth leadership has shifted to China with a GDP that's twice as aggressive as the U.S.

In addition, there's definitely a trend for innovative entrepreneurs like you. Consider the story of Elon Musk. He transformed the once unreachable for a small entrepreneur industry—outer space—and inspired us with a vision to become an interplanetary species and even live on Mars in the near future.

The same is happening with renewable energy, as it rapidly becomes more affordable than coal. The other day, I parked my car under a newly-installed solar-covered parking space with an electric car charging station. While commercial real estate is going mainstream in adopting new technologies, it made my heart sink as I continue to see residential real estate lagging behind. I can't wait for the residential real estate market to embrace solar roofing at an accelerated rate.

And if the concern for Artificial Intelligence (AI) invasion arises, simply remember many bold influential independent enterprises have been implementing multiple layers of security to ensure AI is a safe and open source platform. Plus, there's a growing number of AI platforms to ensure no one can monopolize this powerful technology and to monitor AI the revolution.

Along with Elon Musk, this invasion includes Bryan Jonshon, who journeyed a similar path in creating an internet startup called Braintree, which he sold for $800M. He's now investing in advancing technologies for the benefits of mankind.

Jonshon and Musk are two of my favorite role models (and there are many more). They've proven we can do, or be, or have anything, if we believe it.

You probably already realize that this book is an invitation for YOU to join the forces for good like Jonshon and Musk and become whatever inspires you. Professionally, you can impact and influence people because you're in the middle of the real estate industry,

Why not start right there? A little more passion, a lot more innovation, and inspired actions.

The bottom line is you too can start directing your life as a real estate agent and broker who's leading an innovating, empowering team into the yet to be discovered opportunities of the untapped goodness and income potential – one doubling at a time.

Many things will change, yet change itself will remain a constant force in our lives. And with the technological renaissance and the digital revolution, it will come at a super accelerating rate. Humans will continue to evolve, yet the potential to tap into godlike powers at any moment will remain the same.

Our desire for more and the impetus for the infinite variety of expressions of that power will continue to drive progress. You and I will continue to drive the change and adapt to it by asking unthinkable questions and exploring all kinds of new beginnings like kids in the sandbox. What an exciting promise to live a richly fulfilling life!

Not for the Faint of Heart

The tipping point in this evolution calls for leaders who welcome unthinkable questions, allow ripe answers, and embrace change. That's because it calls for fresh creativity through challenges and opportunities that harness more of our newly-expressed freedom into the joy and thrill of being alive.

Technology will continue to improve our lives, but the essence of human powers will remain the same: the freedom to choose, commit, make decisions, make mistakes, learn, evolve, and repeat the process more quickly. Facilitating the dance between exponential technology and linear human thinking is the task at hand of those who want a more enjoyable ride into the future, including those in real estate. Understanding and appreciating technology with the ability to react decisively will soothe the digital transition and allow us to characterize it as a thrill, rather than a challenge... from a disruption to an exhilaration, and from posing a threat to embracing this evolution time and time again.

The main obstacle in terms of human linear thinking is the trap of attaching and defining our identity to only our jobs... or only our clients... or income or relationships. This fear is rooted in an old worldview cognitive bias that is limiting, untrue, painful, and counterproductive. Deriving our sense of identity from material expressions is a common and dangerous trap that limits our perception of personal power and limits our potential. But it doesn't have to be that way.

Remember my earlier story of how I heard that my neighbor's fiancée shot himself because he couldn't stand the financial pressure of losing his job. Job loss will be common in this transition, and that's why it is important that we start acting as leaders and influencers now. In real estate, we're at heart of this transformation. We have the power, the tools, the experience, the knowledge, and a burning desire to assist society and many individual families through this transition into a new technological renaissance.

Being an Influence starts with the awareness of opportunity, combined with the understanding of critical timing. This leads to a commitment to action and to following the impulse of inspiration.

So, don't wait for bad news from your neighbor, be the influencer and spread the light every day to the best of your ability... one neighbor and one family home at a time.

CHAPTER 20:
WINNING THE GAME OF REAL ESTATE MARKETING

If at this point, you might be asking yourself, "How do I start my journey of becoming a real estate influencer?" Before we answer this question, let's review the three fundamentals discussed earlier.

FUNDAMENTAL #1. Our intuition about the future is linear. However, the reality of information technology is exponential, which makes a profound difference.

> "If I take 30 steps linearly, I get to 30. If I take 30 steps exponentially, I get to a billion."

> —Ray Kurzweil.

WARNING: if you don't continuously double your income, you are falling behind exponentially.

FUNDAMENTAL #2. Before digitization, if you put excellent efforts into your real estate business, you'd see excellent results, and with good efforts, you'd get good results. The digital real estate game has changed exponentially: now with excellent efforts, you'll realize only good results, and good efforts will result in poor results. But those realtors who put in exceptional efforts will get it all.

WARNING: if you don't unleash and leverage your #1 strengths to double your income, you're falling behind exponentially.

FUNDAMENTALS #3. The USD 18.57 trillion GDP (2016) is the result of selling goods and services. The national economy is one giant cash register of buying and selling. Therefore, if you're in business, you must be good at selling. But what drives sales? The answer is marketing.

WARNING: Failing to educate yourself on exceptional marketing on a regular basis will result in losing sales and eventual going out of business. So, ask yourself, "Is my marketing exceptional enough to double my income?" This isn't optional. It's a must.

That brings us to the key asset of your real estate selling and marketing—without which no real estate (or any business) could survive. That key asset is you.... most likely under-appreciated and overworked, hardly over-appreciated by you or your clients and under worked. How can you turn it around?

Let's start with exceptional marketing. The easiest way to define marketing is by defining what it isn't:

#3. It's not marketing like everybody else;

#2. It's not doing what you've been doing;

#1. It's not waiting, postponing, and delaying.

OK, then what is it?

Before I reveal the secret sauce of exceptional marketing, consider the secret in plain sight that all exceptionally marketers are using, but none are openly sharing. And it's not because it is rocket science. It's because most business owners are not ready to take in and integrate this into their business model. However, those who harness it are rewarded by veritable fortunes.

$24,000 per day marketing secret

Recently, my friend paid $24,000 for just one day with a world-renowned marketing authority, who revealed his #1 marketing secret, "If you want to double your income, you must be known for just one thing that you do exceptionally well."

Welcome to the era of personality marketing, the only marketing that can compete successfully with digital real estate. In other words, if you don't effectively market your unique personality in an amplified way, your marketing is ineffective. This impacts your sales and income. In today's acceleration of information overload, a commodity (like everybody else) realtor is becoming exponentially extinct. Yet, celebrity, authority, and expert branding and marketing rooted in your unique personality are on the rise.

To win long-term and double your income game in a digital real estate, you must be known for that one thing at which you excel. But why?

FUNDAMENTAL #4: Prospects come to your office for the buying and selling service, but they stay or leave based on a unique experience from you. If you don't discover, brand, unleash, and amplify your exceptional and unique personality, you'll have a significant obstacle to effective marketing, selling, and survival in the future of digital real estate game.

Consider this: The first line of defense between you and your hot premium leads is average human attention span, which according to Microsoft study has shrunk from 12 seconds in 2000 to a mere 8 seconds in 2013. This explains the 7–second rule of making the good first impression... if you haven't grabbed your lead's attention in 7 seconds... they're moving on to the next realtor!

Put yourself in your prospects' shoes. They just found you online a moment ago, and now you have only seven seconds to make an exceptional, unleashed, branded PERSONALITY first impression. How do you do that?

CHAPTER 21:
THE FUTURE OF MARKETING
AND BRANDING

Personality branding is simple because it's the thing you know best: you. There's no need to pretend you're like somebody else, but... since that one thing that you do exceptionally well is so innate, it's often overlooked. As a result, you don't understand how to use it to gain an unfair advantage. Instead, the question you should be asking yourself, "How do I unleash and amplify my unique personality unfair advantage in 30 days or less?"

The most elegant way to achieve it is by writing a book in 30 days or less. That's why I designed "How to Write A Book in 30 Days or Less" FREE Webinar Training for Realtors that has the power to:

✔ Positioning yourself as a Celebrity, Authority, and Expert. You'll set yourself apart from your competitors and ignite your lead conversion and commissions (Discover how to dominate your market and be the only game in town ...and to be the most-respected, in demand, player in your market!);

✔ Discovering how you can be the realtor who has more business than you can handle, who is helping clients and having fun...while your competitors complain about a lack of work;

✔ Harnessing your invisible power to DOUBLE your income without doubling the amount of work you do. (Not only will you open a new continuous stream of hot leads, but you'll also have much more FREE TIME to enjoy the commissions you're earning);

✔ Avoiding the three biggest mistakes realtors make with lead conversions that cost them clients and commission... and how to immediately solve this problem and turn marketing into an automatic client generation machine!

That's just a small sample of benefits you'll harness from taking attending "How to Write A Book in 30 Days or Less" Webinar training. It gives you the exact roadmap you'll need to run your own ridiculously successful real estate business, enhanced with personality marketing by writing the book and reinventing your brand.

If you're open and serious about taking your income to the exponential level, go to FutureOfRealEstate.co/write

BONUS:
THE SECRET WEAPON
OF LEADS CONVERSION

Rebranding as a Real Estate Celebrity, Repurposing Your Book Content, and Leveraging Search Engine Optimization (SEO).

The Marketing of a Linear Realtor

Marketing your personal brand locally, in your market area, used to be relatively straightforward. It consisted of word-of-mouth recommendations, affixing your name atop a For Sale sign, and perhaps having your portrait grace a supermarket shopping cart. Bus stop benches and diner placemats were popular too. And if an agent had the money, buying a roadside billboard was a good way of reaching a lot of local prospects.

While these marketing mediums remain somewhat effective today, the new digital economy is fast changing that. Over 90% of all home buyers start their search on the Internet. The Internet has become the most important advertising medium for brokers and agents for one simple reason; that's where you find buyers and sellers.

There are expensive ways of leveraging the web to market your personal brand. One of the most popular is Zillow's Premiere Agent program. Zillow attracts millions of prospective buyers and sellers to their website every day. Due to the massive traffic they generate, Zillow charges you a hefty fee to put an agent's name, photo, and contact information next to searched listings on their platform. If a prospective buyer wants more information on a particular listing, they have to contact you, or one of the other agents featured on that Zillow search page. For some agents, this is an important means of increasing their buyer, and sometimes, seller leads. Some agents spend thousands of dollars a month on the Premiere Agent marketing program.

The Marketing of an Exponential Realtor

There is a less expensive and more effective way of marketing on the Internet, and it's called Content Marketing and Search Engine Optimization, or SEO.

And once you've written the book, you can elegantly repurpose its content for SEO Marketing.

This might sound overly complex and intimidating, but SEO is simply about attracting home buyers and sellers to you through posting content strategically on the Internet through blogging. There are a number of ways to increase traffic to you which will result in many more buyer and seller leads. With literally hundreds of millions of websites on the Internet today, you simply can't post something and hope people will find it. You have to develop a strategy to attract them to you.

Strategic blog posting includes repurposing your book's content chapter by chapter and enriching it with SEO. SEO is using relevant keywords and website content to attract links to your content from other websites. That's how you get more people to see you on the Internet. There are several steps you must take to execute an effective SEO and content marketing campaign:

1. Build your own website so you have a presence on the Internet (it's actually easy to do).
2. Use Google Analytics to see where your traffic is coming from
3. Figure out what keywords are the most effective in attracting customers to you
4. Post your own blogs (or hire someone to write them for you) to increase customer traffic
5. Stick with it by creating new content on a periodic basis.

By following those simple steps, you will start exponentially increasing your branding, traffic, leads, and ultimately income, especially if you brand is reinforced by the credibility of the book.

FREE RESOURCES

If you're open and serious about taking your branding and income to the exponential level and double it, this is what you can do next >>

#1. Consider joining FREE WEBINAR TRAINING for Realtors "How to Write the Book in 30 Days or LESS" at:

www.FutureOfRealEstate.co/write

#2. Download FREE PDF "9 Exponential Trends Every Realtor Must Know to Compete with Zillow and Discount Brokerages" at:

www.FutureOfRealEstate.co/free

BIO &
MISSION STATEMENT

Anya Bartholomew, MBA Marketing, has been working and training in the real estate industry as an investor, a realtor and a marketing and branding digital real estate consultant since 2006. As CEO and Founder of DoubleYourIncome.co Digital Real Estate Marketing and Consulting, she has been mentioned in CBS, NBS, Fox News, Google News, Daily Herald and other premium news outlets for her innovative marketing and re-branding strategies. With a MA in Linguistics, certification in NLP and clinical hypnotherapy, Anya designed "How to Write the Book in 2 Days or Less" online (and live) program for real estate agents and brokers, that facilitates radical marketing and branding transformation and results in improved leads conversion and income. Anya trained and worked with realtors, brokers, and investors worldwide on inducing Celebrity Branding leads conversion strategies and digital real estate.

Made in the USA
Lexington, KY
01 November 2018